JUSTICE LEAH WARD SEARS

Justice
Leah Ward Sears

SEIZING SERENDIPITY

Rebecca Shriver Davis

The University of Georgia Press Athens

A Sarah Mills Hodge Fund Publication

This publication is made possible in part through a grant from the
Hodge Foundation in memory of its founder, Sarah Mills Hodge, who devoted
her life to the relief and education of African Americans in Savannah, Georgia.

Set in Garamond Premier Pro by Melissa Buchanan
Printed and bound by Thomson-Shore, Inc.

The paper in this book meets the guidelines for
permanence and durability of the Committee on
Production Guidelines for Book Longevity of the
Council on Library Resources.

Most University of Georgia Press titles are
available from popular e-book vendors.

Printed in the United States of America
17 18 19 20 21 C 5 4 3 2 1

Library of Congress Cataloging-in-Publication Data

Names: Davis, Rebecca Shriver, author.
Title: Justice Leah Ward Sears : seizing serendipity / Rebecca Shriver Davis.
Description: Athens : The University of Georgia Press, [2017] |
"A Sarah Mills Hodge Fund Publication."
| Includes bibliographical references and index.
Identifiers: LCCN 2017009397 | ISBN 9780820351650 (hardcover : alk. paper)
| ISBN 9780820351643 (ebook)
Subjects: LCSH: Sears, Leah Ward, 1955– | Judges—Georgia—Biography. |
African American judges—Georgia—Biography. | Women judges—Georgia—Biography.
Classification: LCC KF373.S417 D38 2017 | DDC 347.758035092 [B]—dc23
LC record available at https://lccn.loc.gov/2017009397

To my father, George H. Shriver,

and to the memory of my brother,

David George Shriver

CONTENTS

JUSTICE LEAH WARD SEARS

INTRODUCTION

How does a young black woman in the Deep South saddled with the twin electoral handicaps of race and sex convince the majority of a state's voting populace to elect her to office four times? How, especially, can she carry off this feat as a Supreme Court justice often obligated to issue unpopular opinions to protect the constitutional rights of minority groups? Good fortune certainly plays a role: our fate is helped or hindered by nature and nurture, by genetics and geography, by the era in which we live. So, too, does our preparation for the lucky break and our recognition of and reaction to opportunity. The choices we make and the skill and effort we put into achieving our goals are at least as important as the luck of the draw.

The title of this book, *Seizing Serendipity*, is meant to evoke the image of one who prepares and positions herself to recognize, appropriate, and exploit accidental good fortune. It is a particularly fitting term for a book about Leah Ward Sears, the first black woman chief justice of a U.S. state's highest court. However, readers familiar with the original meaning of the term *serendipity* will know that the word *seizing* is not entirely necessary. Although often used as a synonym for a lucky chance event, when the word was coined, it encapsulated a richer and more layered idea. English author Horace Walpole concocted the word *serendipity* in a 1754 letter to Horace Mann, the British minister in Florence, when alluding to a "fairy tale" Walpole had read as a child, *The Three Princes of Serendip*. The father of the three princes, a great and powerful king, had decided to endow his sons with more than just power and riches; he also wanted them to be highly educated, perceptive, and wise. So the king hired the best scholars in the land to instruct his sons in a variety of fields and then sent them into the world on a long journey that the king hoped would test and hone their mettle and wits.

Walpole noted that "as their Highnesses travelled, they were always making discoveries, by accidents and sagacity, of things which they were not in quest of."[1] Fortunate circumstances and the princes' astute observations combined, in time, to provide the princes with something other and better than that which they had originally sought, and they eventually returned to Serendip and became three wise and powerful rulers of three different empires.

So in its original form, the word *serendipity* embraces Louis Pasteur's observation that "chance favors the prepared mind." It describes Justice Sears's ability to take full advantage of a lucky break by virtue of the qualities and characteristics she spent her life developing: a sharp mind and sagacious insight, resilience and a capacity for grueling hard work, a relentless drive to succeed, and the ability to appreciate and befriend people as diverse as Ambassador Andrew Young and Justice Clarence Thomas. While Sears frequently managed to be in the right place at the right time, she spent decades preparing for those moments. From Sears's debut as Savannah High School's first black cheerleader to her investiture as chief justice, she was wise enough to perceive and sufficiently prepared and motivated to take advantage of the opportunities that revealed themselves along the way.

This book tracks Sears's life from her birth in Heidelberg, Germany, to her retirement to the private sector from the Supreme Court of Georgia after having twice made President Barack Obama's short list as a potential replacement for retiring U.S. Supreme Court justices. Both a product of her era and ahead of her time on issues such as gay rights, Sears maximized every opportunity she encountered. Affirmative action got her through the door of an Ivy League school, but she used hard work and self-discipline to vault into the top 15 percent of her graduating class. When a seat on the superior court became available in 1988, she possessed the moxie and courage to run for the office and the shoe leather and smarts to win election over her two male rivals, one of whom was the choice of the African American community. In 1992, when Governor Zell Miller made clear that he intended to appoint the first woman to the state Supreme Court, her ingenuity, preparation, and persuasiveness convinced him to leapfrog a thirty-six-year-old black female over the six older and more likely female candidates on his short list despite the fact that he also needed to fill a spot on the lower Court of Appeals, and she had been a trial court judge for only four years.

When the Clarence Thomas/Anita Hill hearings led a tsunami of women to run for and win political office in the Year of the Woman, Sears again defeated a male opponent to retain her seat on the Supreme Court. Two more elections followed in which she faced bitter opposition from at least one man. Each campaign was nastier than its predecessor, culminating in a concerted effort by Georgia's governor Sonny Perdue to unseat her. Despite personal heartache—the horrific treachery of her first campaign treasurer, the death of her beloved father, a painful divorce, the shocking loss of a brother—she persevered. And she prevailed.[2]

CHAPTER I

Climb Every Mountain

After all, the wool from the black sheep is just as warm.
—Sister Margaretta, *The Sound of Music*

The Von Trapp children don't play. They march.
—Frau Schmidt, *The Sound of Music*

Leah Jeanette Sears adored Broadway musicals. Rodgers and Hammerstein's singable, foot-tapping, uplifting tunes provided the background music for the lives of countless young girls born into middle-class families in the 1950s, and with the exception of race, Leah's family fit neatly into the demographic portrayed by the *Father Knows Best*–style television sitcom households of the era. Still, musicals such as *Oklahoma*, *The King and I*, and *South Pacific* tackled such weighty and complicated topics as racial prejudice, slavery, and violence, with the lush and inspiring songs and stories serving as metaphorical spoonfuls of sugar to sweeten life's bitter lessons.[1]

While Leah loved *Mary Poppins* and is still, as she will tell you, a chim-chiminy-cheroo kind of girl, her unequivocal favorite was *The Sound of Music*, and she memorized all the songs made popular by the 1965 Julie Andrews movie.[2] Born in 1955 in Heidelberg, Germany, Leah felt a special connection to the von Trapp family singers, and she yearned to be one of them. So destiny seemed to be beckoning when the ten-year-old girl learned of a casting call for children to appear in the *Sound of Music* at Virginia's Wolf Trap National Park for the Performing Arts. At the time, the family was living in nearby southern

Maryland, where her father, army aviator Thomas Euric Sears, was stationed at Fort Meade, and she begged her mother, Onnye Jean, to take her to try out.

Onnye Jean Sears was a beautiful woman, impeccably turned out and insistent that her children be similarly well groomed.[3] The earliest images that Onnye's youngest child, Michael, has include her driving around Europe in a little Karmann Ghia convertible sporting a fashionable head scarf and dolled up in a Jackie Kennedy pillbox hat as she took her children to visit the museums of Washington, D.C. "Every weekend, my mother would dress us all up, my brothers in suits: little jackets, and ties," recalled Leah Sears. "Black parents used to do that so you didn't look like a ruffian. . . . That was the way we were brought up; you would get all dressed up so you'd command the respect you might not get" otherwise. "Neatness was one of the primary ways for blacks to express dignity and self-definition," explained *Washington Post* reporter Lonnae O'Neal Parker. For that reason, "during the civil rights movement, activists put on their Sunday best, even when they knew their clothes might get spattered with blood." As scholar Evelyn Brooks Higginbotham put it, "The politics of respectability . . . gives you a moral authority to say to the outside world, 'I am worthy of respect. You don't respect me, but I'm worthy of respect. You don't treat me like an equal person, but I know that I am an equal person, and because I am an equal person, I'm going to fight for my rights. I'm going to demand equality. I'm not going to let you treat me like a second class citizen.'"[4]

The day of the audition dawned, and Onnye readied her child for the tryout, dressing Leah thematically in itchy crinolines and tight pigtails, though the ensemble was, for Leah, everyday wear. The little girl's heart pounded with excitement and fear as she and the other children stood longingly before the casting director, who threw a sideways glance in her direction. She watched as he selected a set of twins; she waited as he chose one little blond child after another. Leah didn't make the first cut. Downcast and sick from the stress of both wanting and losing the part, she walked back to the car and threw up. Significantly, neither she nor her family had even considered being deterred by the notion that a ten-year-old black child was unlikely to be selected to play one of the singing children in the Austrian von Trapp family.[5]

Shortly after the audition, Onnye ferried Leah; her older brother, Tommy; and her younger brother, Mike, to downtown Washington. Onnye, an elementary school teacher, routinely took her children on the weekends to educational events, sights, and monuments: "The Smithsonian, all the museums—it was just a treasure trove of cultural activities! So we always went down there. [But on that afternoon], a summer storm came up. We had to take cover. We were near the Capitol, so we just ran in there." As Leah walked into the imposing building with her family, she sensed instantly that something unusual was about to happen. She was right: The corridor seemed to crackle with excitement as Senator Robert Kennedy stepped out from behind a nearby door. Leah recognized him as a famous man whom she and her family revered, and she was terrified. Kennedy walked over to shake hands. Tommy confidently reached out his hand to introduce himself, but Leah was shy; she snatched her hands away and stuck them behind her back. Onnye admonished Leah: Shake the senator's hand! "That's all right," said Kennedy, according to Onnye. "I have a ten-year-old myself." Bending down, the senator swooped Leah into his arms, exclaiming, "You're just a *cute* one!" Then he lowered the astonished and thrilled little girl back to the ground, chatted with the family, and vanished into a waiting elevator.[6]

"He took the time to stop and say hello to this little black family walking through the Capitol, and that blew me away. That absolutely blew me away. And it was a very good feeling," Michael remembered. Five decades later, Leah Sears also recalled with great clarity and emotion that after the rejection of that morning, Bobby Kennedy had chosen her, had embraced her, had lifted her up. Though she did not realize it at the time, the fact that her family never told her that she *couldn't* be a von Trapp family singer combined with the fleeting, kind attention of a celebrated, venerated senator helped further ingrain in the little girl the traits she needed to seize the serendipitous moments yet to come in her life: preparation, courage, perseverance, and hope.[7]

———

Those who know her well say that the key to unlocking the essence of Leah Ward Sears is to know her father, Thomas Euric Sears. A ramrod-straight, rigorously self-disciplined lieutenant colonel who earned degrees in criminal justice, sociology, law, and theology, Tom was one of fifteen children born in Norfolk, Virginia, to William Harvey Sears and Eunice Bell Virginia Mears Sears, a woman fabled to have been "given" to her husband when she was but fifteen years old by a dying aunt for whom she was caring at the time. Just prior to her marriage, Mears had been enrolled in Virginia Normal and Collegiate Institute (which in 1923 became Virginia State College for Negroes), and in later years she was quick to point out to her well-educated children and their offspring that none of them were first-generation college students.[8]

Eunice and William Harvey Sears were hardworking, versatile, and driven: William Harvey raced cars, owned a boxing arena, and labored as an auto mechanic and as a shipwright at the Norfolk Navy Yard. Eunice served as a postmistress while tending a general store: "She'd sell you a slice of pie and then go to the back and mail your package," said Leah Sears, recounting family lore, "and all the kids worked and studied. And every Sunday they went to church. It was just a hard life." William Harvey built the family's home at 919 Washington Street in Norfolk, adding wings here and there as the children kept coming for almost three decades. The ramshackle building was creaky, asymmetrical, and long; the floor shifted when people walked from one section to another, the transition covered by aging carpet.[9]

Born in 1927, Tom Sears was the ninth child, and he learned quickly to fend for himself, as did his next-oldest sibling, Floretta Virginia Sears. Education was an incredibly important component of growing up in the Sears family. According to William Harvey and Eunice, the only way to better one's lot in life was to acquire knowledge and develop skills, and the Sears parents had formidable expectations for themselves and their family.[10] In addition to his many other pursuits, William Harvey Sears, known as "Big Six" for his height, was a member of the Prince Hall Freemasons, the oldest surviving organized body of black men in America.[11] According to Floretta's son, John Charles Thomas, the members of Norfolk's Rising Sun Lodge No. 2 "were big proponents of the spoken word, of rhetoric, of oratory, of poetry. They loved nothing better than someone who could stand and recite." Children and grandchildren were put to the task of memorizing and reciting poetry, and John Charles became Big Six's favorite parlor trick. "When I was around four, he figured out I had a memory. So he put me up to learning poetry, and the first thing he made me learn was William Cullen Bryant's *Thanatopsis*, which, if you've ever seen it, is several pages long. ... These sixty-something-year-old men would come sit on the side porch, and he would say, 'Charles: tell them your poem.' And I would stand there [and recite], 'To him who in the love of Nature holds...'"[12]

Inculcated with his family's regard for education, Tom followed in his mother's footsteps, enrolling in Virginia State College for Negroes. However, he was drafted into the U.S. Army in February 1946, before he could complete his degree.[13]

The aftermath of World War II ushered in an era of tremendous turbulence related to segregation in the U.S. armed services. Civil rights leaders were agitating for integrated military units and had specifically targeted the army, the country's largest employer of minority groups. Although the draft law specifically forbade discrimination against any person on account of race or color, army policy prescribed separate draft calls for blacks and whites, and the institutionalized segregation of blacks and whites had resulted in a host of negative consequences, including low black morale, an inefficient use of personnel, and increased costs to provide separate facilities. Though the tentacles of segregation extended even to the racial separation of blood banks (a policy that had no scientific basis), the army sought to save money by deviating from its segregationist policies and integrating its officer training schools during World War II.[14]

By the end of 1944, the Army Air Forces had a total of 1,303 black officers, and "by that time, the pilot-training program had graduated only 1,374 black pilots, navigators, bombardiers, and others directly involved in flying aircraft." This represented but a fraction of a percent of all blacks in the Army Air Forces, whose 137,806 officers and enlistees accounted for approximately 6 percent of all U.S. military personnel. It was against this backdrop that Thomas Euric Sears was sent to Officer Candidate School and subsequently applied to flight school. While Tom's application was accepted, "he could not have gotten through flight school without a very understanding flight instructor," said Onnye Sears, recalling the story her husband recounted years later. "Because when he went up to do his solo, he was nervous, of course, and he threw up. And many other flight instructors would have just washed him out right away, but this was a very decent man. At that time, blacks were not encouraged to be pilots. White pilots did not want black pilots. They didn't want that competition. So many black guys washed out for much less than that. You know— for any reason. But this guy said, 'Let's do it again.' And they did." Tom, who achieved the rank of lieutenant colonel, flew for the army for twenty-two years and earned the Legion of Merit and the Distinguished Flying Cross during his service in the Korean and Vietnam conflicts.[15]

While Tom was growing up in Virginia and preparing for a military career, halfway across the country in Sand Springs, Oklahoma, Onnye Jean Roundtree was also being raised with a reverence for education, culture, and manners. Elva Thomas Adams Roundtree, Onnye's mother, placed an emphasis on knowledge, words, and geography that rivaled the Sears family's compulsion. Recalled Jewel Roundtree Baker, Onnye's younger sister, "We had this globe that was part of the family. You knew where things were. She made us puzzles before they had the big block puzzles. After a while you just looked at the shape [of the state] and you knew it." Elva saw education as key to personal progress and success and drummed into her children her belief that although being black was an impermanent hindrance, "without education you can go nowhere. Without it you can go no place. There is nothing there for you without it. One day there will be a time when you can't say that the white man is holding you back. You will be holding *yourself* back."[16]

And so the Roundtree children were drilled on geography. They were urged to read books and the *Saturday Evening Post* and *Life* magazines that arrived in the mail. They took turns practicing multiplication on a blackboard hung in the kitchen. They were taught to garden so that they would know how to raise the food they ate. "We'd have our straw hats on, and we each had a hoe we'd put across our shoulder. We'd be single file, and we'd walk down by the levee area where we had community gardens, to our little plot. And we had to go down at least twice a week. We had to chop out the weeds. She was keeping us busy. She was making us know that there was a purpose—we had things to do. We had responsibilities," remembered Jewel.[17]

When the crops were ripe, the Roundtrees had to go pick peas and dig up potatoes, haul the produce home, and prepare it. Young Jewel was sensitive to the comments of the other children who saw the Roundtrees marching down to the garden, and she later asked her mother, "Why did you do that?" Elva replied that they didn't need to care about what others thought. All that mattered was that the Roundtree family knew what it was doing. Jewel later reflected that her mother's lessons had provided tremendous tools with which to tackle life: self-assurance, an ingrained respect for learning and knowledge, and the ability and inclination to assume the mantle of obligation. Elva tasked Onnye with the additional responsibility of helping to raise the younger girls, so Onnye played the role of surrogate mother to Jewel, who later developed a similar relationship with Onnye's daughter, Leah.[18]

Tom met Onnye in Oklahoma during the 1952 World Series. Onnye was twenty-two years old and a newly minted schoolteacher, a recent graduate of Langston University, Oklahoma's only historically black institution of higher learning.[19] While watching the New York Yankees play their crosstown rivals, the Brooklyn Dodgers, the Roundtree children heard a knock at their door. Twelve-year-old Jewel peeked out the window. "Who is it?" asked Onnye. "I don't know," answered Jewel, "but it's somebody in a yellow convertible with a black top!" Onnye's pajama-clad younger sisters ran to answer the door. "During those times, you weren't afraid to just ask people to come in your house. We didn't expect anything to be wrong," recalled Onnye.

The questions cascaded out of Jewel: "Who are you? And where are you from? And what are you doing here?" Tom introduced himself, telling the Roundtree girls that he was from Virginia and was attending Tulsa's Spartan School of Aeronautics. A mutual friend had given him the Roundtrees' address and telephone number and had urged Tom to meet Onnye. Jewel had never before heard of Virginia, so she raced to the back of the house, where the family's globe sat.[20]

Onnye's younger charges were thrilled by the dashing military pilot, with his white silk scarf and leather gloves—and by the cooler full of soda pop in the back of his Buick convertible! Jewel was immediately smitten, but Onnye was a tougher sell. While she accepted Tom's invitation to dinner that evening, she was skeptical about permitting anything other than friendship. "I always thought that he was a little full of himself," she admitted. "He had just returned from Korea, and the reason that he was full of himself, I can see now, is because he was heavily decorated while he was there in Korea. He got a number of medals that he won for bravery. . . . He was only twenty-four years old, and when he went back home to Norfolk, he was a hero. They had a parade for him. I didn't know all of this, of course, but I didn't particularly care for his kind of arrogance. But my sisters did. They loved him."[21]

When it became clear to Tom that Onnye was not coming around in the way he desired, he turned his attention to her college roommate, Martha. The strategy worked: Tom and Onnye married on March 29, 1953. Onnye complained ever after that Tom's antics had damaged her relationship with her friend and that she resented his tactics, but he brushed off her criticism, noting that all is fair in love and war—and that he had gotten what he wanted. "He was very persistent," noted Onnye. "He was persistent throughout his life. And his daughter is a carbon copy of him. She [even] looks like him."[22] According to her cousin, John Charles Thomas, Leah's resemblance to her father means she was "born for good luck," a reference to an old southern prophecy: when a girl looks like her daddy or a boy looks like his mama, the child is destined for good fortune.[23]

Although the military accolades may have encouraged Tom's cockiness, his perseverance was merely a family legacy. Onnye especially admired Eunice Sears's drive, calling her a "top sergeant." Long before Post-It notes were available in stores, the working mother of fifteen made her own by cutting paper into little squares, writing each family member's daily responsibilities on a square, and plastering the notes on the family's refrigerator. "His whole family was like that," marveled Onnye. "Driven. Very driven." Moreover, the Searses played a very active role in the community and saved their pennies so that the children could attend college.[24]

Onnye and Tom experienced their own challenges in raising a family. Tom departed for Germany shortly after their wedding, leaving behind a pregnant Onnye. She joined him in Heidelberg in the summer of 1953, and William Thomas Sears was born the following January. A daughter, Leah Jeanette, arrived just seventeen months later, on June 13, 1955. Black military families were scarce, so Tom and Onnye's children necessarily grew up integrating their environs.

"One of the defining features of my upbringing has been race," declared Leah. "In my very, very early years race was not an issue. . . . I didn't know I was any different from all the kids that I grew up with, and they were all white. . . . I just thought I was like everyone else. . . . I was brown, and they were not as brown." Her perception of the meaning of skin color was further confounded by the fact that her mother is extremely light-skinned, while her father's rich dark hue lay at the opposite end of the spectrum. She recalled thinking that "race was just like eye color" and experiencing "quite a rude awakening" when she realized that it was not so: "I remember when we were in Germany, some of the kids were exploring a cave. [That was] the first time I was called 'nigger.' I didn't know what that meant: 'You're just a nigger.' And I thought, 'Hmmm. That doesn't sound good.' . . . I started to think that my skin color meant something. And it was not good."[25]

The early years in Germany would provide the Sears children with a unique perspective on growing up black in the late 1950s and early 1960s. Michael, born almost eighteen months after Leah during a brief stateside stint in Monterey, California, noted that he and his siblings viewed U.S. events through a European lens as members of a middle-class military family. Dinner-table conversation revolved around topics such as geopolitics, flying, civil rights, and the emerging African continent. Tom loved to travel, so while in Germany, the family toured neighboring countries on the weekends, visiting the Louvre in Paris, the Swiss Miniature Village in Lugano, the Parthenon in Greece, St. Peter's Square in Vatican City, and England's Tower of London—"none of which I truly appreciated," recalled Leah, who pouted her way through many of Europe's glories. The family lived through the 1962 Cuban Missile Crisis "a little closer to the Cold War" than most Americans, according to Michael, living next to the Czechoslovakian border: "They were waiting for the Russians to roll across the border. . . . I knew my dad was somewhere on a tank, pointing east, and even for a five-year-old it's a little bit of a sobering thing. . . . We weren't in Cuba, but we were in Germany, theoretically defending against the Soviet onslaught. . . . I think for all of us—all the kids—that gave us a perspective of how fragile life is [and a way to] understand our place in the world."[26]

That perspective received an American veneer when Tom's tour in Germany ended in 1963 and the family returned to the States on an old World War II transport ship. "We hit New York Harbor and my first impression of America was the Statue of Liberty," recalled Michael. "I knew what [it] was. . . . I knew I was an American, but I was actually coming into this country that I knew nothing of at all, and . . . it was a very moving experience, the shiver I got coming across the water and seeing the Statue of Liberty. Standing by the rails, the whole family was just looking up at this thing . . . that seemed so inviting and so welcoming." Nearly as impressive to the five-year-old was the magical experience of eating at an Automat, a cafeteria with self-serving vending machines, where Michael slid coins into a slot to get a stack of pancakes. So *this* is America, he thought. A land where pancakes come from a machine! Leah's first memories of New York, however, included the less idyllic squalor of Harlem. The drive through the neighborhood represented the first time she associated poverty and injustice with race, and it deeply disturbed her inherent sense of fairness.[27]

The family settled down in Maryland, and Leah began second grade, once again in an all-white school. She engaged in a lot of what she called "civil rights work"—educating her classmates about issues relating to being black. Her schoolmates were "halfway ignorant, halfway sticking it to you all the time," peppering her with questions about her wiry hair. In 1963, the topic of civil rights stood at the forefront of the nation's consciousness. Although the Washington, D.C., and Maryland public schools had quickly integrated their classrooms after the U.S. Supreme Court's 1954 *Brown v. Board of Education* ruling that racially segregated schools were unconstitutional, the states in the Deep South had violently resisted the decision. By the 1963–64 school year, only 1.2 percent of black children in the South attended schools with white children. In his January 1963 inaugural address, Alabama governor George Wallace had vowed, "Segregation now, segregation tomorrow, segregation forever." Martin Luther King Jr. and the Southern Christian Leadership Conference had responded by increasing their civil rights efforts in Birmingham, organizing lunch counter sit-ins, boycotts, demonstrations, and marches. "Day after day, well-dressed and carefully groomed men, women, and children marched against segregation—only to be jailed for demonstrating without a permit." King himself was arrested in April, and during his incarceration, he penned his powerful "Letter from Birmingham City Jail" to explain his actions:

> I guess it is easy for those who have never felt the stinging darts of segregation to say wait. But when you have seen vicious mobs lynch your mothers and fathers at will and drown your sisters and brothers at whim; when you have seen hate filled policemen curse, kick, and even kill your black brothers and sisters with impunity; when you see the vast majority of your twenty million Negro brothers smothering in an air-tight cage of poverty in the midst of an affluent society; when you suddenly find your tongue twisted and your speech stammering as you seek to explain to your six-year-old daughter why she can't go to the public amusement park that has just been advertised on television, and see tears

welling up in her little eyes when she is told that Funtown is closed to colored children, and see the depressing clouds of inferiority beginning to form in her little mental sky, and see her begin to distort her little personality by unconsciously developing a bitterness toward white people; when you have to concoct an answer for a five-year-old son asking in agonizing pathos: "Daddy, why do white people treat colored people so mean?"; when you take a cross country drive and find it necessary to sleep night after night in the uncomfortable corners of your automobile because no motel will accept you; when you are humiliated day in and day out by nagging signs reading "white" men and "colored"; when your first name becomes "nigger" and your middle name becomes "boy" (however old you are) and your last name becomes "John," and when your wife and mother are never given the respected title "Mrs."; when you are harried by day and haunted by night by the fact that you are a Negro, living constantly at tip-toe stance never quite knowing what to expect next, and plagued with inner fears and outer resentments; when you are forever fighting a degenerating sense of "nobodiness";—then you will understand why we find it difficult to wait.[28]

On June 10, as George Wallace stood on the University of Alabama campus physically and symbolically barring black students from entry, President John F. Kennedy federalized the Alabama National Guard and issued a proclamation ordering the governor to cease blocking a federal court order to integrate. Late the following evening, Medgar Evers, the Mississippi field secretary for the National Association for the Advancement of Colored People (NAACP), was murdered in his Jackson driveway. On August 28, Martin Luther King Jr. delivered his eloquent "I Have a Dream" speech at the March on Washington, speaking to a crowd of more than two hundred thousand, stretched out like a "thick carpet of people on both sides of the half-mile reflecting pool." Just three weeks later, however, four black girls were killed in a Sunday-morning bombing at Birmingham's Sixteenth Street Baptist Church.[29]

The Sears family's first year back in the United States came to a somber conclusion when President Kennedy was assassinated on November 22, 1963. Leah recalled her teacher "coming into class, saying, 'Children! Children! The president has been shot!' By the time I got home, my father was just standing in front of the TV set." When the president's body lay in state, Onnye Sears took her children "to the Capitol to see the casket. We were standing out there for hours in a sea of humanity. We just stood there with tears streaming down." At around that time, Michael began "to feel the tension of who I was in America. All of a sudden, I realized that people were excluding me. . . . It wasn't a feeling I had grown up with. It wasn't a feeling that I had had a long tradition with. It just kind of hit me around '63, '64—that I'm a black American."[30]

Also around this time, Leah Sears began to think about becoming a civil rights attorney, a goal that led her to order law school catalogs. However, Leah noticed that those catalogs showed page after page of young white males but no law students who looked like her. "'I felt like I was a second class citizen,' she recalled. At that moment, a determination set in. 'I knew I had to be somebody. And if that was to happen, I had to make things change.'" Although this oft-told vignette seems as apocryphal as the story of George Washington and the cherry tree, Leah's aunt, Jewel Baker, confirms the tale: "Most people are intrigued by stuff like that, but for Leah, it was just natural. She's always been focused."[31] In the black community, lawyers were that era's prominent agents of change. The NAACP Legal and Educational Defense Fund had waged a decades-long fight to end school segregation that reached its apex in the *Brown* ruling just a year before Leah's birth. In 1961, the NAACP's inaugural director-counsel and the nation's most prominent civil rights attorney, Thurgood Marshall, had become "the first black American to serve on the U.S. Second Circuit Court of Appeals."[32] In 1962, when Leah was seven, NAACP attorney Constance Baker Motley, one of the few black women attorneys at the time, had helped James Meredith become the first black student admitted to the University of Mississippi.[33] Leah's black middle-class upbringing and her cognizance of the events of the day no doubt drove her somewhat precocious childhood ways, but other stories of her tender years are much more far-fetched: she did not, for example, memorize civil rights opinions, and she did not entertain the notion of becoming a judge until shortly before she had children of her own. And while, as widely reported, a grade school report on Constance Baker Motley was indeed one of her inspirations to become a lawyer, she cannot recall whether she or someone else wrote the paper.[34]

Leah's father encouraged the notion that people were obligated to foster change for the better, and he required his children to commit to memory a family motto he had coined, borrowed partially from the Boy and Girl Scouts: "duty to God, duty to country, duty to self through scholarship, good works, dignity, and pride."[35] Privately, though, he worried that his ambitious daughter, whom he saw as a female version of himself, would be "doomed to be disappointed in a world where young women . . . especially young black women, were expected to iron out pillow cases, not the laws of the land." Nonetheless, Tom urged his daughter to think expansively, to dream of something larger than herself, to eschew being a small person living a small life. He boosted his daughter's confidence with a rare compliment: when his sons were fighting over which of them was a better writer and speaker, he announced that Leah was better than both of them. "I'll never forget my father saying, 'I love your sister's voice. I love her articulation and her diction. And I'm soothed by it.'" The event affected her profoundly.[36]

In 1964, Onnye got a teaching job, and she and Tom enrolled the children in the Prince George's County school where she was employed: "I had the idea that I could look after them better and know what was going on, and we could all go to school together and come back," explained Onnye. The children were less than enthusiastic about having a parent in such close proximity: her classroom was directly across the hall from Leah's. Moreover, in Prince George's County as in many communities, even when school districts were formally desegregated, blacks and whites lived in different areas, leaving many schools predominantly or wholly populated by students of one race. For the first time, the Sears children were surrounded by black classmates. Beaver Heights Elementary School also provided Leah with her first mentor, fourth-grade teacher Ethel Stewart, who was also the first African American teacher Leah had ever known. "She was the first person who, outside of my family, took me in, told me I was smart, encouraged me," Leah recollected. "She liked my voice. . . . I don't speak the vernacular; they call it Ebonics now. She liked to have me read for the class."[37]

The Sears siblings returned to an otherwise all-white school the following year, when Onnye took a job teaching at Lanham Elementary School. "The first day we started school, when we walked through the front door, I remember all the kids saying things like, 'Niggas! Niggas are arriving! We got Niggas in the school! Niggas! Oh, God—Niggas!' And I just won't ever be able to forget that," Leah recalled.[38]

Across the Potomac, Leah's cousin, John Charles Thomas, took a similar tack when he became one of twelve black students to attend Maury High School in Norfolk, Virginia, under a freedom-of-choice plan in 1965, more than ten years after the *Brown* decision. As John Charles explained, in response to the Civil Rights Act of 1964, which gave the federal government authority to withhold funds and file suits against segregated school districts, "The southern schools said, 'You want integration? Any black kid can leave his neighborhood school and go to any white school and any white kid can leave his neighborhood school and go to any black school. They have freedom of choice. We're integrated. That's it!' The black teachers weren't buying it, and so they basically got some of us in a room and said, 'Y'all got to go to a white school.' 'Whyyyyy?' 'Because we're fighting for integration, and if you don't go, it's going to fail. You've got to go.' 'Yeeeeesss maaaaa'am.'" Such plans did little to end segregation, since few black students chose to attend white schools as a consequence of "lack of information, intimidation, lack of space or seats at the alternative school, and a lack of free busing or transportation." After 1968, federal courts generally rejected the gambit as an ineffective tool for promoting desegregation.[39]

As a child, John Charles had only "episodic" interactions with Tom, Onnye, and their brood: "They just were from another world. I mean, we were kind of down and dirty in the funky South in streets without sidewalks, and into town would come Uncle Tom in his army uniform, driving some cool car. . . . When we knew they were coming, we would climb trees all around the neighborhood and have lookouts. . . . The first cousin who saw them would yell, 'Here he comes!' We would form this party and run down the street behind the car. They were something like royalty. . . . They lived in exotic places. They were overseas and in other states. . . . We were Norfolk, Virginia, southern colored kids. [They were] well mannered and well raised and well groomed. . . . We were *agog*!" The Thomas family's thin financial resources and largely absent father provided a sharp contrast to the atmosphere in the Sears household.[40]

Tom's family traveled to see his kin on Christmas or on Thanksgiving, a holiday on which his mother, who claimed a birthmark in the shape of a turkey, contended she was born, though the family Bible records Eunice's birth date as November 24, 1895, the Sunday before Thanksgiving that year. One Christmas, Leah proudly recalled, her father "flew Santa Claus" in a helicopter, landing him "on a parade field so that Santa . . . could get out and hand out gifts to the kids. He was a black pilot flying Santa! My father looked so handsome and dapper with his wings on his uniform—just beautiful!" John Charles was delighted when the Sears family arrived for one visit in a small plane piloted by Tom, who also thrilled the youngest children by cradling them in one of his huge hands and "flying" them toward the ceiling.[41]

Tom's play was peppered with drills and demands, however: "Troopers! Troops! Help your grandmother clean off the porch, and pick the crabgrass because we are going to the beach later today if it's done on time," he would order. "Uncle Tom, we're done!" "You missed something over there. For that, we're going to be delayed for an hour!" he would bark. John Charles recalled that Uncle Tom taught his nephews to swim by getting into the water and saying, "'Swim to me.' But he would keep backing away. We would be swimming [as hard as we could], and he would just keep disappearing.... And then he would say, 'What's nine times nine?' 'Eighty-one!' someone would gasp. 'Good, trooper!'"[42]

In the mid-1960s, the Sears family moved to Savannah, where Tom was stationed at Hunter Army Airfield. While there, Tom became involved as a leader with the Boy Scouts. Russ Williams III was working to become an Eagle Scout, and Tom became the counselor for Russ's Citizenship in the Nation merit badge. Other counselors had routinely signed off on merit badges when Russ fulfilled the minimum requirements, and he thought that this badge would be no different. But when Russ walked into Tom Sears's office, however, the officer stood, firmly shook his hand, grilled him on the badge's prerequisites, and then asked the boy if he knew the preamble to the Constitution. When Russ said that the preamble was not among the requirements for the Citizenship in the Nation badge, Tom said, "Well, I'm not going to pass you off on this merit badge until you can learn the preamble to the Constitution. Come back next week and know it."

The stunned Boy Scout returned the following week, but his stumbling attempt to recite the preamble was again rejected, with the lieutenant colonel thundering, "No, no! This is not acceptable.... You don't understand at your age, but it's *important* that you understand the Constitution." After two more failed attempts, Russ finally realized that Tom was not going to budge and finally memorized and recited perfectly the words: "That's the thing that stuck with me all these years. He would not accept anything less than my best." Decades later, after Tom's death, Russ wrote to Leah that the lessons from that boyhood encounter had reached far beyond his ability to narrate the preamble to the Constitution: "I hope it is some comfort to know that your father's legacy lives on in the lives of people like myself who were influenced so posi-tively by his example and leadership." "That's my father," Leah acknowledged. "And that's me."[43]

Leah, too, was involved with scouting, and she, too, refused to take the easiest path. On one occasion, she was supposed to bring a "sack lunch" for an outing to a Girl Scout camp on Rose Dhu Island, off Savannah. Instead of packing a sandwich and cookies, Leah lugged along an uncooked Cornish hen and an empty commercial-sized vegetable can into which she had punched two holes. She then skewered the poultry on a makeshift spit rod, fashioned the contraption into a rotisserie, and roasted her lunch over charcoal as the other Girl Scouts dined on cold cuts. Leah stood out from her sister scouts in yet another way: she and two other black girls belonged to a primarily white troop, and they became frustrated when a white camp counselor pooh-poohed their fear of wet hair—for Leah and the other African American girls getting wet "would make my hair lock, and I'd have to pull it hard, and I had no con-ditioner, no blow dryer: I'm at camp! So I can't deal with this. It would start to rain, and the three little black girls would start running for cover and [the counselor would] say, 'Stop it now! Water never hurt anyone. It's no big deal.' But it is. Damn it—we'd been in the beauty shop for three hours Saturday; it's only Sunday, and this is going to kill [our hair for the] next two weeks!" Among African Americans in the mid-1960s, "straight hair was not only the preferred look but a marker of one's position in society. Light skin and straight hair still represented wealth, education and access to the upper echelons of society." Leah and many of her peers thus devoted copious amounts of time and money to using harsh chemical hair-straightening products, and their efforts would be undone if their hair was exposed to humidity and regained its natural kink. Though certainly more subtle than overt racial discrimination, such cultural misunderstandings were still significantly troubling and problematic.[44]

One of the other African American Girl Scouts, Pamela Monroe, was, like Leah, the daughter of an army officer. The two girls attended Savannah's Bartlett Junior High School, where they and Leah's brothers were the only blacks. The four endured indignities seemingly invisible to the whites in their world. For example, when the Girl Scouts performed a production of Louisa May Alcott's *Little Women* in the spring of 1968, the lead roles went to white girls, while Leah served as the narrator and Pam was cast as a maid: "We have to be realistic," reasoned the troop leader. Such slights could be overlooked, but others caused more serious wounds. On April 4, the girls were rehearsing the play when they learned of the assassination of Martin Luther King Jr. "That's good," remarked one of the Girl Scouts. "He was just a troublemaker." Though Leah is often pragmatic about forgiving personal slights, that memory still made her furious nearly half a century later.[45]

According to Pam, the Monroe and Sears families provided their children with the tools needed to cope with being black in a white world: self-esteem, confidence, and a sense of worth even in the face of occasional inequity. "The context didn't build my character," declared Pam. "It was my family environment, the sense that [I was] important. We had solid values. [My parents would tell me], 'You're going to be successful. You're going to college. Study. Hard work pays off.' So when you have that type of shield, it doesn't matter where you go." The same was true in the Sears household.[46]

The two families' six children played as hard as they worked: they swam, rode bikes, and held a carnival, charging admission to the Sears's backyard. The boys played football at Hunter Army Airfield, and Pam and Leah were on the cheerleading squad, each proudly donning a blouse with a Peter Pan collar and a sweater sporting a big green *H*. Leah continued the sport, becoming the first black cheerleader at Savannah High School. The role was not a natural fit for her, however: "You had to be *cute! Perky!* And I was not perky." A shy, studious young woman with a sense of purpose, Leah felt rather out of place. And in fact, the caption on the yearbook photo of the squad misspells her last name: *Tears*.[47]

Leah, like other teenagers, at times yearned for adventure and independence. On one occasion, she told her parents that the cheerleaders were taking a trip to Atlanta. She neglected to mention, however, that only the older squad was going—Leah's ninth-grade team was not included. She nevertheless joined the older girls on the train, and when she stepped off in Atlanta, she was smitten: "I loved Atlanta. I loved how pretty everybody looked, how gracious everybody was—this was going to be my home!" At Rich's department store, she ensconced herself in the Magnolia Room, integrated just ten years earlier, ordered a pot pie, and marveled at the sophisticated women in their fashionable clothes enjoying a "ladies' lunch."[48]

But that evening, as she was "acting stupid" during a basketball game at

Georgia Tech's Alexander Memorial Coliseum, she saw her father staring at her across the court. She returned with him to his hotel room in the Americana, where she would pay the price for her wild spree: "I'm so disappointed in you," he said. A self-described "good girl," Leah instantly dissolved in tears. No further punishment was required.[49]

Leah also attempted to assert herself with her mother. In 1969, when Onnye's beloved younger sister, Jewel, arrived for a visit with her newborn son, Billy, Onnye delightedly announced, "I want to buy Billy his first new suit." "How much is that going to cost?" demanded Leah. "That doesn't matter," said Onnye. But Leah countered that one-fifth of the family's wealth belonged to her, and she did not want her money spent on a suit. Not surprisingly, Onnye did not agree and did precisely as she wished. Leah and Jewel were nevertheless close, and that summer, Leah accompanied Jewel back to San Diego. On July 20, Jewel, little Billy in his swing, and Leah watched Neil Armstrong and Buzz Aldrin land on the moon. "This calls for champagne!" cried Jewel, and Leah readily agreed. After checking with her father, aunt and niece toasted Apollo 11's fulfillment of President Kennedy's dream.[50]

The hit songs of that summer included Johnny Mathis's "Love Theme from Romeo and Juliet," and Leah was one of many teenage girls who developed a crush on the singer. When she told her aunt, "He's so handsome," Jewel responded that he "went the other way." It was the fourteen-year-old's introduction to the idea that men could be attracted to men, though she couldn't quite grasp the concept. At the time, societal homophobia and laws criminalizing homosexuality discouraged people from being openly gay, and Mathis did not publicly acknowledge his homosexuality until 1982. But the summer of 1969 saw the birth of the gay liberation movement when patrons at New York's Stonewall Inn rioted after a June 28 police raid on the gay club. Though that movement would profoundly affect Leah's career, at the time, all she knew was that she liked Mathis and his music. She also sang along with "Good Morning Starshine" and "The Age of Aquarius," two hits from the rock musical *Hair*, which had premiered on Broadway just weeks after Martin Luther King Jr.'s murder in 1968. The lyrics preached peace and love, harmony and understanding, just as Robert Kennedy did when he broke the news of King's assassination to a shocked crowd in Indianapolis: "What we need in the United States is not division; what we need in the United States is not hatred; what we need in the United States is not violence and lawlessness, but is love, and wisdom, and compassion toward one another, and a feeling of justice toward those who still suffer within our country, whether they be white or whether they be black." However, Kennedy also acknowledged that violence, lawlessness, and disorder were ongoing. Indeed, not only did riots erupt in cities across the country in the wake of King's death but Kennedy himself was assassinated just two months later, news that Leah learned when her teary, red-eyed mother woke her in the middle of the night. With the nation bitterly divided over the war in Vietnam and the struggle for civil rights, Republican presidential candidate Richard Nixon "trumpet[ed] the slogan of 'law and order' all the way to the White House" while pledging to pull troops out of Southeast Asia.[51]

By that time, Leah and millions of other African Americans had begun to question American involvement in Vietnam after witnessing reports regarding the nation's first "television war" on the nightly news. President Lyndon Johnson had initially been popular with civil rights activists for maneuvering the Civil Rights Act of 1964 and the Voting Rights Act of 1965 through Congress, but much of that support had disappeared as a consequence of Johnson's escalation of the war. Disproportionate numbers of African American soldiers were dying in what had begun to look like an unwinnable conflict, and prior to his death, the charismatic King had become increasingly outspoken in his opposition. In addition, boxer Muhammad Ali was stripped of his heavyweight title in 1967 after he refused to be inducted into the U.S. Army. In 1968, trusted CBS anchorman Walter Cronkite grimly concluded that "it seems now more certain than ever, that the bloody experience of Vietnam is to end in a stalemate." However, many black soldiers and their families did not share King's antiwar sentiments. When Leah asked her older brother, Tommy, "Should we be there?" he explained the domino theory: a communist victory in one nation would quickly lead to a chain reaction, meaning that the United States had to support noncommunist South Vietnam against communist North Vietnam.[52]

But like most fourteen-year-olds, Leah's day-to-day interests primarily featured less weighty subjects. Her memories of her summer in California feature cherries, the beach, Sea World, and the San Diego Zoo, where she felt a seed of discomfort at seeing animals in small enclosures. She also loved shopping with her aunt: "We went to a department store, and I bought her this fantastic burgundy mini two-piece outfit with platform shoes," Jewel recalled. "And at the end of July, when it was time for her to return home, . . . her father saw her in that miniskirt, he [said]: 'Ohh hooo—that's kind of short, Lady! Kind of short, there!' But [Onnye] Jean talked him into allowing her to keep it." Leah increasingly began asserting her independence, often through her personal style, and it was not the last time Onnye would have to run interference for the teenager blossoming into a woman in the summer of 1969.[53]

CHAPTER 2

An Intellectual Feast

Sentry-like o'er lake and valley towers her regal form,
Watch and ward forever keeping, braving time and storm.
So through clouds of doubt and darkness gleams her beacon light,
Fault and error clear revealing, blazing forth the right.
—Wilmot M. Smith and Archibald C. Weeks,
Cornell University Alma Mater

The Pulitzer Prize for the best photograph of 1969 featured a young black man wearing a bandolier of bullets and brandishing a rifle aloft as he emerged from Cornell University's student union. The minister of defense of the Afro-American Society (AAS), Eric Evans, was leading more than eighty other members of the group, some of them carrying rifles or shotguns, out of Willard Straight Hall, which they had occupied for thirty-six hours on April 18–20. Amid the marches, demonstrations, sit-ins, and sundry other disruptions of universities and colleges nationwide in the 1960s, the Straight takeover was infamous for introducing guns into the equation.[1]

Cornell was on the cutting edge of higher education when it came to minority recruitment. Its Committee on Special Education Projects (COSEP), established in 1963 as the Committee on Disadvantaged Students, had particularly targeted inner cities in its attempt to expand Cornell's black student population. The initiative succeeded, raising the number of undergraduate minority students from 8 in 1963 to 250 by the 1968–69 academic year. However, many of these students came from backgrounds quite unlike those of the typical white

Cornell student, and they felt alienated on the campus of fourteen thousand. Though the AAS, formed in early 1966, originally included whites, "younger members moved in a separatist direction in fall 1966, when the new influx of students with Black Power and black consciousness beliefs changed the tone of the organization." As the *New York Times* noted in a profile of Cornell's president, James A. Perkins, "the changes he set in motion at the university . . . led to its own transformation. The increased presence of Negroes on the campus . . . stirred some racism by white students and responsive militancy and violence by blacks."[2]

The Straight takeover began when approximately one hundred students evicted about forty cafeteria and janitorial staff workers and thirty slumbering guests visiting Cornell for Parents' Weekend. The action was precipitated by two incidents. First, the university had attempted to discipline six black students involved in a demonstration four months earlier. The students had sought a separate black college within Cornell as a remedy for the frustration felt by inner-city COSEP recruits who perceived that they were studying subjects that were irrelevant to their lives. The students refused to recognize the jurisdiction of the student-faculty disciplinary board, contending that since the demonstrations were a political act directed against the university, it was a party to the dispute and thus ineligible to sit in judgment. The takeover also constituted a response to a cross burning on the steps of Wari House, a black women's cooperative established in 1968 as a reaction to cultural misunderstandings, hostility, and dorm confrontations between black and white women. The cross burning occurred shortly after the student-faculty board on student conduct reprimanded three of the students involved in the December demonstrations and was accompanied by fire alarms set off in dorms and university halls, keeping firefighters, police, and security officers in frenzied motion until the early morning hours of April 18. The bedlam resumed that evening, intensified by two bomb threats.[3]

Once the AAS had taken over the Straight, the men served as sentries and sent the women to the kitchen to cook breakfast.[4] At that point, the students were not armed. The Students for a Democratic Society, one of the most prominent student activist organizations of the 1960s, set up a picket line in front of the building and demanded that the administration repeal the reprimands and pardon any crimes committed during the takeover. At one point, twenty-five members of the white Delta Upsilon fraternity entered the building through a window to "liberate the Straight" but were beaten back with anything the occupiers could grab. The AAS then began smuggling in guns they had purchased earlier in the term in response to threats against the organization as part of "the philosophy and strategy of 'self-defense of the black community' that was now an integral part of the Black Power movement." Although the AAS intended the weapons for self-defense only, their presence generated panic and led the administration to accede to virtually all of the students' demands. University officials agreed that the dean of the faculty would recommend a nullification of the judicial proceedings against the black students, not to press criminal or civil charges against the occupiers, and to investigate the cross burning.[5]

The image of the gun-toting students emerging from Cornell's student union building electrified the nation and further stimulated anger, anguish, and controversy on campus. As one young black woman complained in an exasperated interview with the *New York Times*, "Guns, guns, guns; that's all they can talk about. . . . Don't they understand we're talking about the legitimacy of black students on a white college campus, our survival as an entity in a hostile environment?" Gloria Joseph, the director of COSEP, explained that "much of the frustration of the black students is focused on the curriculum, that they feel is geared to white America," a condition she described as "the whole question of racism in education."[6]

In 1976, when Leah Sears graduated from Cornell, the university's inaugural black yearbook, the *Ethos*, was dedicated to these young revolutionaries. During the 1969 occupation of Willard Straight Hall, however, she was navigating her way through Wilder Junior High School in Savannah, Georgia, oblivious to the turmoil rocking her future alma mater.

When the Searses moved to Savannah in 1967, Tom and Onnye bought a house at 38 Monterey Avenue, becoming the only black family in a predominantly Jewish neighborhood. Leah's parents had chosen that locale because they wanted their children to have the best possible home environment and education. Tom "did not believe in private schools," Onnye explained, "so I looked for the better [public] schools. And usually they were in the area where we had purchased a home, because we made sure [to] get our money's worth in buying a home. [Wherever there was] a very good home and a good neighborhood, usually you'd find a good school."[7]

In the summer of 1970, before Leah started tenth grade at the high school, Onnye and Tom Sears decided to take their children on a trip around the world. Tommy, Leah, and Michael initially tried to beg off because of cheerleading and sports commitments, but after consulting with their coaches, Tom insisted that they were going. The plan was to take advantage of the military's "space available" flight privilege, also called Space A or military hops, which enables service members, retirees, and their families to travel on U.S. military aircraft when the planes aren't filled. The Searses traveled to Charleston, South Carolina, to begin their journey, but after several days of waiting for a flight that had enough room for all five members of the family, Tom elected to purchase tickets to Germany and pick up a Space A flight in Spain. They traveled for about a month, visiting numerous countries, including Pakistan, India, Thailand, and Japan. As Onnye recalled, when military flights were not available, "we had to pay our way. Sometimes we rode commercial flights, sometimes we rode the train." She also remembered that the kids had fun, although "they only started enjoying themselves about halfway through the trip." In Thailand, they visited Pam Monroe, Leah's old friend from Bartlett Junior High and the Girl Scouts, whose family had moved there. In Japan, they traveled to Osaka, which was hosting Asia's first World Exposition. Tom had learned Japanese while serving during the Korean War, and he was in his glory in Japan. Not only could he read the train schedules, but other tourists mistook Tom for a celebrity and asked him for his autograph. When Tom obliged, Onnye would say, "'You've got to be kidding. They think you're somebody else!' I mean, he had that attitude about himself."[8]

What most struck Leah about the trip was the unfamiliar swirl of humanity: "I was never so bowled over with the museums. It was the people. . . . The people cooking on the street . . . the poverty . . . the cows walking through the streets. . . . I'm more into people and the way they live and adapt to environments than the great art and the great buildings."[9]

The Sears family's travel experiences set Leah and her brothers apart from most of their peers, and this sense of separation was exacerbated after tenth grade, when she was forced to switch high schools. For nearly fifteen years after the U.S. Supreme Court's *Brown* decision outlawing school segregation, many districts across the South, including Savannah, had failed to implement anything more than token integration, using freedom-of-choice plans and other strategies to prevent black and white children from attending school together. In 1969, the Court finally declared that it would tolerate no more delay, ruling that all school systems immediately needed to integrate; two years later, the Court held that when schools were racially unbalanced as a consequence of residential segregation, busing was an appropriate way to achieve integration.[10]

In 1962, thirty-six African Americans had filed suit against the Savannah–Chatham County school system, seeking to force it to comply with the law and operate a truly unitary school system. For the remainder of the decade, local officials and the state of Georgia stalled, seeking a way to avoid meaningful integration. On June 30, 1971, however, the U.S. District Court for the Southern District of Georgia approved a busing plan that would bring Savannah–Chatham County's public secondary schools into compliance with a "long and unbroken succession of cases" decided by the federal courts that made "it clear that any law or regulation of a state, county or municipality requiring or furthering racial discrimination in the public schools violates the federal Constitution." On August 31, as the school board continued to search for ways to circumvent the law, the court ordered the immediate integration of the public elementary schools on the basis of a busing plan that the members of the Board of Education had discussed but "could not and would not bring themselves to approve."[11]

The two court orders sparked massive protests. On September 1, Lieutenant Governor Lester Maddox, an ardent segregationist, appeared at a rally at Savannah's Memorial Stadium and urged the nearly five thousand people in attendance to refuse to submit to "forced busing." Maddox called the school desegregation decisions "a part of a Communist plot" and exhorted Governor Jimmy Carter and fellow state officials to defy the judicial orders.[12]

A former president of the Savannah–Chatham County Board of Education called for a boycott of the public schools on Friday, September 3, the first day of the 1971–72 school year, and about fifteen thousand students—more than a third of Chatham County's secondary students—did not attend that day. Although students returned to school over the next few weeks, the unrest continued as parents blocked the entrance to one school, burned an effigy of the current school board president, and made their children lie down in the road in front of school buses. In addition, opponents of integration appealed the district court's desegregation order, but in November, the Fifth Circuit Court of Appeals affirmed the decision. A special session of the General Assembly subsequently passed the Savannah–Chatham County Freedom of Choice School Assignment Law in yet another attempt to skirt the federal court's orders, but the court instructed the Board of Education to ignore the legislation, remarking, "It is difficult to conceive how anyone could suppose for one moment that a state legislature can, in effect, amend the Constitution of the United States as it is construed by the highest Court and nullify orders of federal courts enforcing the Equal Protection provision of the Fourteenth Amendment. Such may be the law of the land in Alice's Wonderland. It is not here."[13]

The atmosphere of hostility continued through the school year, and students predictably split into factions at Beach High School: the new students who were bused in belonged to one group, the old Beach High students belonged to another, and things were so disorganized, it was "really too much of an adjustment for some of them." A rock-throwing incident between students riding on Beach High and Savannah High buses left a twelve-year-old girl with a broken nose, and the Board of Education had to ask for federal marshals after some four hundred black and white students at Jenkins High School refused to report to class and instead threw rocks, bottles, and bricks at each other.[14]

As black children who had previously attended the white high school, the Sears children did not fit in with either group at Beach. Recalled Leah, "They took [my] neighborhood and said, 'This neighborhood of white kids is going to integrate this all-black school.' So I'm riding the bus to go integrate! It was just bizarre." She continued, "The blacks were fighting the whites, and the whites hated the blacks. There were fights every day, and nobody was learning anything.... The blacks jumped on me for being 'too white' ... and the whites didn't like me because I was black. It was just a mess." It was a difficult time for Leah: "I had white friends in high school, and that was unpopular.... I didn't fit in with whites and I was [reviled] by blacks. I had a very, very good [white] friend in high school that I dropped eventually because it wasn't popular to be with her. And I know she was hurt. But I was trying to figure out my way." Leah again became a cheerleader at Beach High School, and on one occasion, her mother remembered, two teammates threatened to drop her because "they thought she acted white." The Sears children's frustration was compounded by the fact that, as Michael Sears put it, "we were a little bit ahead of the curve in terms of academics. [I imagine] Leah was bored."[15]

The experience was so wretched that Leah chose to attend summer school in 1972 so that she could graduate in August, just two months after her older brother. "As I walked across the stage, I remember slipping. I had these slick shoes and I slipped, and I thought, 'Well, hell, this doesn't matter!' And it didn't. My goal was just to get out."[16] And Leah had a destination firmly in mind: Cornell University. Law school remained her ultimate and unwavering goal, and not only was Cornell geographically far away from home, it received state support. Tuition for the College of Human Ecology was low enough that she could acquire a relatively inexpensive education from an elite institution. In fact, as part of the school's effort to attract minorities, she received a scholarship that covered her tuition.

Leah's parents had encouraged her to attend Spelman College, a historically black college for women in nearby Atlanta, but she had different ideas. Looking through Cornell's catalog, she was delighted by the "smorgasbord of offerings" and was eager to immerse herself in what her mother called the school's "Bohemian" atmosphere, which would enable her to discover new worlds and savor an "intellectual feast."[17]

The New York Legislature had chartered what is now Cornell's College of Human Ecology in 1925 as the New York State College of Home Economics. Although the name changed in 1969, the "Home Ec" association persisted, and Leah "was always embarrassed that I was at Human Ecology—but I *loved* it. It tickled my practical sense. . . . It wasn't so esoteric; it was people solving people problems." Eleanor Roosevelt was an early supporter of the college and its founders and pioneering codirectors, Martha Van Rensselaer and Flora Rose, and in 1929, when Roosevelt's husband, Franklin, was serving as governor of New York, she used her influence to help the school obtain funding for a building. Leah viewed Cornell as a progressive advocate of coeducation and women's rights. There was much to support that impression: Ithaca, New York, was just forty miles south of Seneca Falls, where the world's first women's rights convention was held in 1848, and in 1872, Cornell became one of the first eastern universities to admit women. Exactly one hundred years later, when Leah enrolled as a freshman, Cornell formally established a women's studies

program in the College of Liberal Arts and Science. The program had origi-
nated in 1970 as the female studies program, one of the first of its kind in the
country.[18]

After receiving her acceptance from Cornell, Leah discovered that most
incoming minority freshmen would be attending COSEP's summer orientation
program. Eager to meet other African American students, she applied for and
gained admission to the program. So in the summer of 1972, Tom and Onnye
Sears drove nine hundred miles north, Michael in tow, to deliver to Cornell
their only daughter and her pink steamer trunks jammed full of clothes and
other necessities. The family stopped to visit Onnye's sister, Jewel, in Virginia,
where Leah displayed a little too much exhilaration at the prospect of her
impending freedom. According to Jewel, Tom responded "in a very stern,
warning voice, 'Be careful, or you won't get to Cornell! We'll turn around and
go back to Georgia.'"[19]

Leah took heed. But when she and her parents arrived at Mary Donlon Hall,
where she would be living for the summer, Tom was outraged to discover that
the dorm was coed. He announced to his daughter, "Baby, you're going to have
to leave this place because you're not going to live in a dormitory with boys!"
Leah tried to explain that nearly all of the dorms were coed and that Cornell
had a severe housing shortage, but Tom was adamant—at least until Onnye and
Leah managed to calm him down. After settling Leah into her room, Onnye
and Tom left for home, with Tom breaking down and sobbing over losing his
"baby," something Leah did not learn until years later.[20]

Shortly after fall classes started, Leah was standing in the Noyes Community
Recreation Center when she heard a familiar voice exclaim, "Leah! What are
you *doing* here?" There stood Pam Monroe. The two young women discovered
not only that they both had received scholarships but also that they both were
living on the fifth floor of Sperry Hall. Pam had graduated a year early from the
International School of Bangkok, where a recruiter from Cornell had entranced
her with a photo of the central campus's 173-foot McGraw Tower.[21]

Unlike Leah, however, Pam had not known about the COSEP orientation
program. In fact, Pam had received almost no information from the university
beyond her acceptance letter and through a miscommunication had arrived
on what was actually the first day of classes. Stunned, Pam had spent two days
obtaining a dorm assignment and frantically attempting to register for classes.

When she saw her dear friend, Leah at first seemed to be "a mirage of sorts"; then an enormous sense of relief washed over Pam. Leah, too, was delighted. Pam had written from Bangkok to tell Leah that she would be attending Cornell, but the letter did not arrive until well after they were ensconced at the university. For the rest of their undergraduate days, the two friends, "nerds— good girl types," according to Leah, "protected each other [and] looked after each other."[22]

In 1972, Aretha Franklin won a Grammy Award for her album *Young, Gifted, and Black*, and the sense of jubilation expressed in the title song accurately represented the world that seemed to be opening up for Leah and other African American women at the time. Shirley Chisholm became the first black woman to run for the presidency, and attorney and Texas state senator Barbara Jordan became the first black woman elected to the U.S. Congress from the Deep South.

The Twenty-Sixth Amendment, enacted in 1971, gave eighteen-year-olds the right to vote. Leah leaned toward support for the incumbent, President Richard Nixon, though she was still just seventeen, too young to cast a ballot. As a military brat, Leah preferred the strength she saw in Nixon over "doves" like Nixon's opponent, Democrat George McGovern. Moreover, she was impressed by Nixon's dramatic February 1972 trip to the People's Republic of China—the first such visit by a U.S. president since the communist country's establishment in 1949.

Two years later, however, Leah watched, transfixed, on a small black-and-white television as Jordan, the junior member of the House Judiciary Committee, tolled the death knell of Nixon's presidency in her "Statement on the Articles of Impeachment": the president had attempted "to subvert the Constitution" when he "counseled his aides to commit perjury, willfully disregard the secrecy of grand jury proceedings, conceal surreptitious entry, [and] attempt to compromise a federal judge, while publicly displaying his cooperation with the processes of criminal justice." But before she turned her attention to arguing on behalf of Nixon's impeachment, Jordan had uttered some words that resonated strongly with Leah: "Earlier today, we heard the beginning of the Preamble to the Constitution of the United States: 'We, the people.' It's a very eloquent beginning. But when that document was completed on the seventeenth of September in 1787, I was not included in that 'We, the people.' I felt somehow for many years that George Washington and Alexander Hamilton just left me out by mistake. But through the process of amendment, interpretation, and court decision, I have finally been included in 'We, the people.'" Watching Jordan, Leah recalled, "I was so proud!"[23]

Leah was overwhelmed by the riches that Cornell offered: "Not one library, but *six* libraries! You could just go and sit in the library and read any book you wanted on any subject!" In addition, the school offered numerous other avenues for education, including some that she "could never [have imagined], everything you [could] want. Lectures, all different kinds of courses. Women's studies! Black studies!" After receiving only mediocre grades during her first semester, Leah buckled down and began spending weekend days studying in the library. Carrying her lunch, she would commandeer a carrel and stay all day, pausing occasionally to gaze out the tall windows or to listen to the carillon housed in the nearby tower that had so captivated Pam. She felt lucky to be at Cornell, and she realized that she would need to become a grind if she wanted to accomplish her goals. Leah gravitated toward the unfamiliar, hungry to learn as much as she could about the world outside her "small cocoon." A comparative religion class exposed her to Mormonism and to Pentecostalism. One seminar brought her first contact with an openly gay man; she also met a woman who shared her husband with other women—a "swinger." Leah enrolled in "small classes of weirdness," thrilling to the lessons of nationally prominent professors such as Urie Bronfenbrenner, whose groundbreaking research on the impact of environment on child development had influenced the formation of Head Start in 1965. Leah's interest in the health of children and families and her intellectual curiosity about societies and cultures subsequently became lifelong themes.[24]

In addition to the women's studies program, Cornell added several other diversity-supporting entities during this time. The Gay People's Center had been launched in the spring of 1972, and the Africana Studies and Research Center had been created in the wake of the 1969 takeover of Straight Hall. According to Leah, "All the black students of my era often went [to the Africana Center] to learn, often for the first time, about the history of the black man in the world."[25]

The university had been walking a tightrope over a racial chasm since the late 1960s, when it responded to complaints that African American students were having difficulty adjusting to Cornell by pairing COSEP students in dorm rooms and housing them within "hailing distance of each other." However, the racial conflict in the dorms continued, with black students complaining that they could not study effectively because so much of their time and energy was spent "fighting the alienation, frustration, and fear they encountered in an essentially white University." The university then sought to solve the problem by housing seventy-two COSEP students together in half a dorm. In 1972, Cornell designated that dorm, North Campus Hall 10, as a special living unit for students concerned with "analyzing and solving the problems of underdeveloped countries, particularly those of African descent." The Ujamaa Residential College took its name from the idea of family conceptualized by the first president of Tanzania, Julius Nyerere. The dorm, embellished with African prints and pictures of Langston Hughes and Marcus Garvey, was one of Leah's favorite haunts, though it also served as a lightning rod for controversy during her college years.[26]

Soon after its founding, Ujamaa came under fire for its membership selection process. The New York State Board of Regents, which supervises all of the state's educational institutions, ordered the university to integrate all of its racially segregated facilities, and the University Senate's Minority and Disadvantaged Interests Committee began an investigation to see whether Ujamaa was impermissibly refusing to admit white students. During a tense question-and-answer session, representatives of Ujamaa stressed that it constituted a community of students sharing common interests, just as Risley Residential College functioned as a community for students interested in the creative and performing arts: "Ujamaa is open to all students interested in studying developing communities," stated one resident. However, the resident added, no whites had applied to live there. In January 1974, the Board of Regents ordered the dismantling of Ujamaa as a consequence of its de facto segregation. In December 1974, after sustained resistance from the university and two tours of Cornell's five special residential communities by members of the board, the regents blinked, accepting a university plan to monitor the application and selection procedure for the communities.[27]

Having grown up attending largely white schools, Leah found it refreshing to be among "my own, free to express myself and not have to constantly be filtering all the time." She rarely interacted with white students and sat at the "black table" during meals. She developed a "*pissed* passionate" need to learn as much as possible about her African American heritage, angered that "through ignorance and the way society worked" she had been sheltered from and denied that treasure trove of knowledge. "Race was *everything*" during those years.[28]

The emerging campus and community publications of that era confirm her observation. *Black View*, a minority newspaper partially financed through a work-study arrangement with COSEP, released its inaugural issue in 1973, and in 1975 a student organization founded *Eclipse* magazine, an "organ of communication to express the politics, culture, and creativity of the minority communities to the larger Ithaca, Ithaca College and Cornell audiences." The journal's title sought to suggest the "triumph of darkness and hue . . . the ascendency of something once obscured."[29] One year later, Leah's graduating class published *Ethos*, Cornell's first minority yearbook, which reflected the events, organizations, and activities that had affected and were affiliated with Cornell's minority population.[30]

Women, too, were starting to create a larger space for themselves on campus and in the world. As Leah began her second year at Cornell, the law school appointed its first female professor, Patricia Anne Barald. At the time, women comprised only 15 percent of the law school's student body and 7 percent of the total Cornell faculty.[31] Earlier in 1973, the U.S. Supreme Court had handed down *Roe v. Wade*, its controversial landmark opinion on abortion, and the New York Assembly's Banks Committee was in the midst of testimony from a series of women who were routinely unable to get loans from banks and credit institutions without a male cosigner. One woman complained that her bank required her husband to cosign her application for overdraft privileges on her checking account even though she had worked longer and earned more money than he. What particularly upset her, however, was the fact that she was employed by the same bank.[32] In 1974, Quill and Dagger, Cornell's eighty-one-year-old senior honorary society, admitted its first female members; the following year, Pam and Leah were tapped to join the ranks.[33]

Despite Aretha Franklin's exhilarated tone, however, black women also faced a daunting and often conflicting set of quandaries and frustrations created by their double burden of gender and race. A conference at Cornell on "Dimensions of Black Womanhood," sponsored by the Africana Studies and Research Center and the Black Sisters United, stressed a "need for black nationalism and the rejection of the women's lib movement." At the gathering,

Malcolm X's widow, Betty Shabazz, endorsed the notion advanced by another panel member that women were "the completion of man" and that women's role was to "stimulate our men to create." Shabazz emphasized that black women would "gain nothing by maintaining a division between themselves and their men."[34] Pam Monroe, who had been selected to introduce Shabazz, was not predisposed to accept the entire theme set forth by the panel but acknowledged that "there is a truth in it. There is nothing to gain by division between anybody." Pam pointed out that one of Shabazz's primary complaints was that "the women's movement was not inclusive enough of black women, that some of the issues that black women face were not being addressed by the women's movement. . . . I think her [point] was that white women were sitting on pedestals and they wanted to get into the workforce. We've never been on a pedestal."[35] Shabazz broached a topic very familiar to black women: as African American journalist Lonnae O'Neal Parker pointed out in her 2005 book on the challenges black women face, "It wasn't until I was an adult that I even understood that some women considered paid, outside-the-home work optional. Because for the black women in my world, work wasn't an option at all. . . . Black women and field work and house work and paid-outside-the-house work simply go too far back."[36] Leah echoed that observation: "We're not stay-at-home moms. . . . It's just not in our consciousness. And I don't think many [white] feminists understand that whether to work outside the home or not has never been an option for black women."[37]

Leah and Pam further strengthened their identities as black women during their sophomore year, when they moved from Sperry Hall to Wari House, a three-story cooperative near the Africana Center. Wari House was founded in 1968 by black female students who sought relief from constant clashes with their white counterparts in the dorms, confrontations that often arose as a consequence of misinterpretations and cultural differences.[38] For Leah, Wari House encouraged bonding, support, and affirmation among black women, but her motive for moving there was not quite so lofty: Wari House was inexpensive, and she would be able to have a room to herself during her junior year.[39] In addition, moving to north campus meant that she would no longer have to struggle up Libe Slope through the winter snow to get to her classes, a Herculean chore that in 1870 felled the first women student at Cornell, Jennie Spencer.[40] Pam, too, was eager to leave behind the strategically placed ropes that the residents of the west campus dorms grasped to climb the hill, and she was thrilled to be living with Leah in a double room that seemed enormous compared to the dorm.[41]

Onnye worried that her daughter, a sheltered, "shy little southern girl," would be overpowered in an environment where the other women hailed primarily from large cities. And indeed, most of her housemates at Wari had come from the ghettos of New York City and were familiar with sex, drugs, and confrontation. One woman decided that she wanted Leah's room and abruptly threw Leah's belongings into the hallway. But Leah had changed, too: no longer the "shy little southern girl," she now wore combat boots and an Afro, and her years at Wari House were not only empowering but also proved key to her education.[42]

Leah and Pam maintained their studious habits, though distractions abounded. Provost David Knapp's 1975 plan to dilute COSEP's functions by centralizing admissions, recruiting, and financial aid into one office and give academic departments responsibility for overseeing academic aid for minority services spurred a furious backlash. Black students and faculty members suspected that Cornell was trying to promote the failure of minority students and remove them from the university. Knapp argued that minority education needed to become an "integral part of Cornell's academic life" or it would never be more than an "add-on to the whole." But the students weren't buying the administration's justifications for change, and a wave of sit-ins, rallies, marches, and angry debates ensued. Of particular concern was the plan to phase out the Learning Skills Center, which specialized in tutoring minority students in the concepts and skills needed for academic success, provided a forum for minority students to voice their opinions, and offered counseling specific to their concerns and needs.[43]

In October of that year, the Trustee Ad Hoc Committee on the Status of Minorities recommended the dispersion of COSEP's functions, triggering even more demonstrations. An alleged rape of a black woman in November sparked the fifth and most explosive protest that semester, with about three hundred students marching through campus and then cornering the president and provost in the administration building for two hours. Their demands included stationing a security guard at Wari House. The rumors of the rape were linked with the changes made to COSEP, and the administration was accused of fostering an atmosphere that encouraged and permitted violence against blacks.[44]

Leah found herself caught up in the frenzy, and the experience constituted a significant turning point in her life. She watched police officers try to protect the protesters "from themselves" and witnessed three white male students suffer a beating for breaking the protest line: "They weren't doing anything, and the black guys beat them up. And I was so *pissed*." Her sense of justice prompted her to leave the protest. While she and Pam still appreciated the serious issues that needed to be addressed and rectified, Leah's more natural inclination was to approach friction with composure and conciliation. But "those weren't times where people like me were listened to. It was 'Burn, baby, burn!' and 'Let's kick their ass!'" People generally saw her as rather conservative.[45] The demonstrations continued into April when black activist Stokely Carmichael, addressing a crowd from the steps of Straight Hall, condemned the university for dismissing a black assistant financial aid officer. Two hundred students responded by sweeping through Day Hall on a window-breaking rampage and then staging a ten-hour takeover of the building, almost seven years to the day after the armed takeover of the Straight.[46]

However, by this time, Leah's energies were concentrated elsewhere. Leah was in love with Love, but she still wanted a prenup.

CHAPTER 3

Love, Life, and Death

The old idea that we are the Second Sex, that we will follow
a man to the ends of the earth, is giving way to a more balanced
and appropriately self-centered orientation.
—*Our Bodies, Ourselves,* 2nd ed.

Love Collins, a cadet at the U.S. Military Academy, first met Leah Sears when he traveled the two hundred miles from West Point to Ithaca to compete in a track meet. Eighteen-year-old Leah was having what she later described as an "Ujamaa moment": her hair was wrapped and tied in a colorful head rag to convey her connection to her African roots, as many African American women did on college campuses in the 1970s. However, as Leah added, "we didn't know" that "African women don't wear things like that."[1]

Her image stuck with Love, who wrote to Leah the following year when he would be participating in another meet at Cornell. They planned to get together at Wari House, and seeing the triple jumper "bounce, bounce, *bang*" piqued her interest. He had the credentials she wanted: he was a college-educated man from an intact family and he spoke "the king's English," a quality of great importance to her. Her heart melted completely when she learned that Love's mother had died when he was thirteen, leaving his father to raise Love and his six younger siblings. Leah was very taken by the fact that his father had kept his family together and had plans to get them through college. Leah and Love soon began spending their weekends traveling back and forth between Cornell and West Point. On Friday afternoons, Leah would hop in her car, crank up Earth, Wind, and Fire, and meander down Route 17 through the Hudson Valley. Once Love was relieved of his duties at six o'clock, they would return to Cornell together.

Love and Leah began to plan a future together, and those weekend drives became a series of negotiations. Leah insisted on a prenuptial agreement. Neither of them had much money, so their arrangement was not financial. Rather, it was a series of items on which Leah felt they needed to agree. "Let's talk about Item 3 on the prenup," she would begin, brandishing her pen. "How many children?" "Two, no more than three." She would take his last name only by attaching it to hers with a hyphen. She would fulfill her dreams of law school. Her career would not take a backseat to his. "I pulled the idea out of those semifeminist, hang-tough kind of '70s books like *Our Bodies, Ourselves*: I'll marry you, but I'm not giving my soul to you. I typed it up and made copies. He signed it, and I signed it."[2]

Leah was a product of her times, surfing the second wave of feminism that swelled in 1963 with the publication of *The Feminine Mystique*. Written by Betty Friedan, founder of the National Organization for Women (NOW), the book exposed the general frustration and unhappiness middle-class suburban American housewives were widely experiencing in their confining "proper" role as wife/mother/homemaker, a social construct that denied women the ability to explore other avenues of fulfillment. The first wave of feminism, launched by the 1848 Seneca Falls Convention, was most visibly fronted by upper-middle-class white women fighting for suffrage, a goal that was realized in 1920 with the passage of the Nineteenth Amendment to the U.S. Constitution. The second phase, which included an emphasis on sexuality and reproductive rights, drew in more African American women, but even so, Sears recalls that black activists at Cornell in the 1970s considered NOW the province of white, upper-middle-class women and expected black women to postpone their liberation to support their men. *Our Bodies, Ourselves*, a seminal book about women's bodies, health, relationships, and sexuality, emerged from that second wave of feminism. The seed for the manuscript was planted in a discussion group on women and their bodies at a 1969 women's conference in Boston, grew into a course for women on women, and blossomed into a book that featured chapters on pregnancy and menopause as well as information on rape, self-defense, birth control, abortion, and lesbianism. The sections offered excerpts from personal stories, such as "Black Single Women on How Their Relationships with Men Have Been Damaged by Racism and Sexism," and discussed the many types and facets of monogamous and nonmonogamous relationships. "For those of us who decide that marriage *is* a very deep and important relationship for us," stated the section on "The Experience of Being Married," "our marriage will be far better if we feel that it is our clear choice rather than our only alternative or our life-defining duty." Leah's prenup was her way of clarifying and memorializing her conditions for entering into what was, for her, a deep and important relationship.[3]

Leah Jeanette Sears and Love Collins III married on July 3, 1976, at Butler United Presbyterian Church in Savannah, with Jewel Baker and Pam Monroe as matron and maid of honor, respectively. And although both Leah and Love legally changed their surnames to *Sears-Collins*, the *Savannah News-Press* labeled the young bride "Mrs. L. Collins" in the announcement of their marriage. Just two pages later, the paper printed an interview with Marabel Morgan, an Ohio State University dropout and former beautician whose 1974 best-seller, *The Total Woman*, had just been released in paperback. The book showed wives "how to serve their husbands better," offering suggestions such as "Wear baby doll pajamas, white boots and a cowboy hat when you greet hubby on his return from the grease pit, assembly line, rolling mill, or office." Feminists clearly faced some significant societal obstructions, although progress had definitely occurred on the racial front. Just eleven years earlier, the *Savannah News-Press* would not have printed the Sears-Collinses' wedding announcement at all since they were African American.[4]

Ignoring *The Total Woman*'s recommendations, Leah Sears-Collins immediately began law school at Duke University in Durham, North Carolina, where she had received a full scholarship. Love remained stationed at Fort Benning in Columbus, Georgia, and after just ten weeks, Leah found that the separation put too much strain on their union: "I put marriage first, which is, I think, what I've always done, even for the so-called radical liberal I'm supposed to be. I thought we were not going to make it starting out like this." Leah decided to put her dreams of law school on hold for a year so that she could join Love in Georgia and be a military wife. Determined to spend that interim working at a "cool job" where all the "smart people" were, Leah briefly became a cub reporter for the *Columbus Ledger*, though she had poor typing skills and no previous experience in journalism. She obtained the position by showing up at the newspaper's office almost every day and asking the managing editor, Baxter Omohundro, if there were any openings. After a few weeks, Omohundro tired of turning her down and offered her an internship. Leah jumped at the chance, perfectly willing to start at the bottom when a job excited her.[5]

Journalism and journalists indeed possessed a certain panache at the time. Two years earlier, President Richard Nixon had resigned after *Washington Post* journalists Bob Woodward and Carl Bernstein uncovered his role in the June 1972 Watergate burglary and the subsequent cover-up. Moreover, 1976 saw the release of *All the President's Men*, in which Hollywood stars Robert Redford and Dustin Hoffman portrayed Woodward and Bernstein. Leah Sears-Collins's beat was somewhat less glamorous, though she did love being in the newsroom. She covered Fort Benning events and wrote mostly feature articles, offering advice about poison ivy, wasp bites, and rats. She contributed to coverage of Elvis Presley's death and conducted several informal surveys, one of which polled shoppers about their reactions to some controversial comments made by the U.S. ambassador to the United Nations, Andrew Young, who later became instrumental in initiating Leah's judicial career.[6]

Leah Sears-Collins enrolled in law school again in the fall of 1977, choosing Emory University in part because it was located only one hundred miles from Columbus. Classmate and close friend Rebecca Zimmerman, whom Leah teasingly called *Zimmerperson*, recalled that "between being black and being a woman, I think [Leah] always felt she had to work harder than everybody else. She just felt this was what it was going to take for her to be successful, and she always saw herself making a difference and having an impact."[7]

During this time, women were flocking to law school, in large part as a result of Title IX of the Education Amendment Act of 1972, which prohibited sex discrimination in academic institutions receiving federal funds, and the Women's Educational Equity Act of 1974, which funded educational opportunities for women. In 1971–72, prior to the enactment of Title IX, first-year female enrollment in law schools was around 12 percent. That fall, the law school at Virginia's Washington and Lee University finally opened its doors to women, becoming the last law school in the nation to do so. By 1977–78, Leah Sears-Collins's first year at Emory, women accounted for more than 30 percent of new law students, and that number continued to climb over the next two decades, nearing 50 percent, where it remains. Unlike many of its counterparts, Emory School of Law, which opened in 1916, had never prevented women from enrolling. In fact, the law school's 1917 entering class was one-third female: Eleonore Raoul, the first woman admitted to Emory University, was one of the three students.[8]

Black law student enrollment was a different story. Unlike some other southern educational institutions, Emory's charter and bylaws did not explicitly reject students on the basis of race. However, when the school sought to integrate in 1962, it had to file a lawsuit to strike down state laws that revoked the tax exemptions of private institutions established for white persons that subsequently admitted black students. The Supreme Court of Georgia noted that state law also required that private institutions with tax-exempt status be open to the general public. "As we view these two provisos, the first one, standing alone, means that no private school is entitled to a tax exemption unless it is open to the general public without regard to race or color; and the second one, standing alone, means that a private school would not be entitled to a tax exemption unless it operated on a segregated basis as to the white and colored races. Since there is unquestionably an irreconcilable conflict between these two provisos, they completely neutralize and destroy each other," said the court. A few weeks after the court's decision, Emory Law School admitted its first black student, Ted Smith, who enrolled in the evening program.[9]

Emory then began active efforts to attract black students, and in 1966 it instituted an innovative admissions strategy. Law school officials regarded the Law School Admission Test (LSAT) as a culturally biased, inadequate measure of black students' academic potential and devised the Pre-Start program as an alternative. Emory recruited Pre-Start students from historically black colleges and universities based on prelaw advisers' recommendations. The students participated in regular blind-graded summer law classes and were offered admission if they earned a cumulative average of 70 or higher. In the program's first year, nine of twelve Pre-Start students were admitted to the law school. They had undergraduate grade point averages comparable to those of other entering students, but their mean LSAT scores were considerably lower: 358 versus 545. Nonetheless, six of those nine students earned law degrees. The Pre-Start program ended in 1972, giving way to the national Council on Legal Education Opportunity program and Emory's creation of a special scholarship fund for black students.[10]

Despite law schools' efforts at affirmative action and retention, blacks comprised roughly 5 percent of the first-year enrollment at law schools nationwide during the 1977–78 academic year, and the minority attrition rate was high. As a minority within a minority, Leah Sears-Collins was a member of a very small universe. Saddled by the double handicap of gender and race, attributes that are often viewed through a discriminatory lens, Leah felt impelled to work feverishly to prove her worth and realize her goals. That perception accompanied her throughout her life, enabling her to smash many barriers as well as to empathize with others struggling to win acceptance for characteristics over which they have no control.[11]

Leah Sears-Collins began acting on her ambitions to change the world when she was placed in the Columbus Regional Office of the Georgia Legal Services Program in the summer of 1978. The eradication of domestic violence was another cause championed by second-wave feminists in the late 1960s and 1970s, and Leah sought to contribute to the fight against spousal abuse, which she had witnessed among military families. Many people saw nothing abnormal when husbands hit their wives: abuse that "was so acceptable back then!" Leah recalled. "But not me. Never me. It wasn't going to be my daughter, and it wasn't going to be me." Sears-Collins received a grant from the Law Students Civil Rights Research Council that provided financial support for her summer in Columbus, when she studied the problem and organized a community support system for spousal abuse victims. She created and disseminated literature and held a series of public forums and open houses at which people could talk about domestic violence. She spoke with the lawyers at Fort Benning and made a number of local media appearances to raise awareness about the problem. She obtained nearly twenty detailed case studies and then drew on them to write a thesis about the crime's causes, effects, and solutions. The organization she founded, the Columbus Battered Women's Project, continues to operate today as the Columbus Alliance for Battered Women, a nonprofit corporation that provides temporary shelter and counseling for abused women. The interest in and dedication to the health and well-being of children, marriages, and families evidenced by that long-ago summer job subsequently shaped and informed her jurisprudence.[12]

While in law school, Leah also served as a resident adviser at Emory, a job that added to the considerable demands on her time. Nevertheless, when she graduated in 1980, she ranked in the top 15 percent of her class. Her cousin, John Charles Thomas, attended the ceremony: "When she finished law school, her daddy called me and said, 'Charles, you've got to come to her graduation.'" When John Charles tried to beg off as a struggling young attorney just five years out of the University of Virginia Law School, Tom declared, "Charles, you're the only lawyer in the family. And you need to be here." So he emptied his wallet to buy the graduate a Parker fountain pen and treated the Sears family to a celebratory dinner.[13]

Leah Sears-Collins accepted a job at Alston, Miller & Gaines, a silk-stocking Atlanta firm. Although she initially planned to become a civil rights attorney, as John Charles Thomas observed, "there are different ways to get at it." Recalled Sears-Collins, "There were very few blacks going to big firms like that. I was smart enough to be asked to come, and I thought that I should go if asked. It wasn't just for money; it was an opportunity that few blacks were getting. Moreover, "there were no black female lawyers, so I had no mentor, no one to model myself after."[14] Perhaps not surprisingly, she hated her new job. "I went with the biggest, baddest, coolest law firm without even thinking, 'Does this fit with my lifestyle?' I just thought, 'This is where I should be because this is where *everyone* wants to be.'" But after five years of wearing muted, stodgy suits and working on federal antitrust cases, Leah realized that a large southern law firm was not where *she* wanted to be. "I felt suffocated. I felt not appreciated. I felt dumb for reasons that aren't legitimate other than the fact that I could not be who I could not be. I couldn't do it their way. I wasn't made to do it their way. It was very closed, not diverse, not all that progressive. If you didn't fit into the club, you didn't do well. It was hard, and they didn't try to make it easy. It was upper-class, upper-crust southern white guys. And I wasn't that." Nor was she alone in her feelings of isolation. Years later, the *Fulton County Daily Report*, Atlanta's daily legal newspaper, accused the city's legal community of racism, poor recruitment efforts, and a lack of mentors: "In a city that is 67 percent black and led by politicians who were leaders in the civil rights movement

... blacks at major Atlanta law firms are admitted in small numbers and then are rarely nurtured in their professional development. . . . The isolation felt when an associate is one black among 100 white lawyers often becomes intolerable, forcing young black lawyers to leave. The racism is often subtle, sometimes unintentional. A black associate tells of being mistaken for a messenger. . . . A client, flush with cash after a public offering, tells a black partner he is 'nigger-rich.'" In 1981, Leah Sears-Collins and nine other black women decided to combat that sense of Otherness and build strength in numbers by establishing the Georgia Association of Black Women Attorneys, a group dedicated to women and children's issues and increasing black female representation in the judiciary and in public offices. Sears-Collins served as the group's founding president.[15]

Another rare opportunity presented itself when Leah was talking to Atlanta mayor Andrew Young at a cocktail party and he urged her to become a traffic court judge on the City Court of Atlanta. Young, who had "spent the 1960s in the eye of the storm of the civil rights movement," was himself a high-profile breaker of barriers. In 1964, after Young had earned a reputation as a deft intermediary between black civil rights activists and the white business community, Martin Luther King Jr. named Young executive director of the Southern Christian Leadership Conference. In 1972, he was elected to Congress, becoming the first black U.S. representative from Georgia since Reconstruction. Several years later, after throwing his support to Jimmy Carter's presidential campaign, Young was tapped to serve as U.S. ambassador to the United Nations, becoming not only the first African American to serve in that role but also, at age forty-four, the youngest person to hold the ambassadorship. Young brought to the international community the ideals of the civil rights movement but took heat for making a number of controversial remarks to the press and for meeting with a representative from the Palestine Liberation Organization. Concerned that the negative publicity might impede the peace process in the Middle East, he resigned in 1979.[16]

Young returned to Georgia and was elected mayor of Atlanta in 1981. Prior to his conversation with Sears-Collins, his daughter, Andrea, less than two months younger than Leah and a graduate of Georgetown Law School, had advised him that he needed to start women judges out early if he ever wanted to see one sitting on the Supreme Court. At twenty-seven, Leah was a prime candidate. "We need some youth down there," Young told her. Stunned and thrilled by Young's suggestion, Leah began preparing her dossier. The Superior Court of Fulton County was responsible for sending the mayor a list of suggestions for the part-time judgeship, so she made an appointment with its chief judge, Joel Fryer. "I went to lay out my credentials. I had a package: my résumé and some writings. And the first thing he said was, 'Is the mayor going to appoint you?' I said, 'What do you mean?' He said, 'Do you have the heads-up? Is the mayor going to appoint you? We want to make sure whoever is on the list is who the mayor is going to appoint!'" Leah was "shocked with his honesty and shocked at the political process and shocked that he didn't want to hear that I graduated from an Ivy League school with top grades." And with that, the pragmatic Fryer introduced the idealistic young woman to the practicalities of politics.[17]

Leah Sears-Collins found that she loved the swirl of humanity coming into traffic court and relished dealing "with all of their silly excuses: 'I didn't see it coming!' or 'There was a yellow light!' It wasn't serious stuff. Most of it was just a wonderful chance to connect with people." She discovered, too, that she liked the authority that came with the bench. Early on, one woman came into court sobbing, "I got this ticket. It wasn't fair. And I'm going through a divorce and I just—I can't afford twenty-five dollars right now!" "Just leave the courtroom," Judge Sears-Collins responded. "I'll dismiss the ticket. It's probably not right to dismiss it. But this is not a good time for you right now. Go home. Go home. Go home. You get a break." But Leah also realized the potential for abuse. "I liked being able to step in and do that. But you have to work not to abuse your power. You don't want to walk around like a [dictator] or you can go nuts. And many politicians do go nuts. . . . People are always blowing smoke, and you can begin to believe it."[18]

Within a year, Leah was preparing for another change in her life: a baby. Her pregnancy coincided with the publicity for the third *Star Wars* film, *Return of the Jedi*, which was released on May 25, 1983. Leah had seen the first two movies and was enchanted with the similarities between the names Anakin Skywalker and Anakin Sears-Collins. Love Sears-Collins disagreed, exploding, "Hell, no! Grow up. I'm not naming my son after a fictional character in a *Star Wars* trilogy!" Leah then combed through a book for three-syllable names beginning with *A* and came up with *Addison*. Love was much more amenable to that suggestion, in large part because he had just finished reading about Addison Emery Verrill, a celebrated zoologist. When Leah gave birth on June 7, 1983, at Georgia Baptist Hospital, she and her husband named their son Addison Love Sears-Collins.[19]

Leah Sears-Collins was not overly fond of babies: "I don't like the one-on-one with blobs of people who can't interact with you. I didn't like the early years of my own kids, where you have to be saddled with diaper bags and milk. I found that very burdensome. They just sit there and stare at you. I start to like them when they can give you something back!" In contrast, she was energized and excited by her interactions with people in her courtroom. Moreover, when Addison was a year old, he was rushed to the hospital, but as a young associate, Leah was stuck in a meeting and could not leave. So when Judge Thelma Wyatt Cummings left the City Court to serve on the State Court of Fulton County, Leah seized the opportunity to serve as a full-time judge.[20]

Leaving a lucrative position at Alston & Bird for traffic court was a big risk for the ambitious attorney who still wanted to change the world. As U.S. Supreme Court justice Clarence Thomas observed, "Daring to take a step down from a prestigious firm and begin the judging process is a commitment! That is believing—because it may begin and end right there." Her leap of faith made the thirty-year-old Sears-Collins the youngest full-time judge ever to serve on a City Court of Atlanta. In September 1985, when Young swore her in as a full-time judge of the City Court of Atlanta, the city's African American newspaper, the *Atlanta Daily World*, noted that her father had earned a law degree from Atlanta's John Marshall School of Law and that both of her brothers were attending Stanford Law School. Moreover, in April 1983, Governor Charles Robb had appointed John Charles Thomas to serve as the first African American justice (and the youngest justice ever) on the Supreme Court of Virginia.[21]

The following year, Leah and Love Sears-Collins welcomed a daughter to their family, naming her *Brennan*, after U.S. Supreme Court justice William Brennan, whom Leah greatly admired. Though Leah also thought highly of Thurgood Marshall, the first African American justice, she "didn't feel comfortable" naming a girl *Marshall* or *Thurgood*. As Leah worked to teach good manners and civility to her two young children, she realized that many other people needed that guidance: "When I was in the traffic court, I didn't like the way people were coming to court dressed. I sent a memo to the other judges, saying 'We need a dress code. I can't adjudicate these people's cases if they show up with toothpicks sticking out of their mouths, do-rags on, short-shorts, flip-flops, and halter tops. You're not going to get the best out of me because of the first impression I get.'" After Atlanta's seven full-time judges implemented a dress code, Leah Sears-Collins took her quest to garner respect for the City Court to the national level. "I have always believed that the term 'lower court' is a misnomer because in many ways, these courts have an impact on the lives of citizens, both collectively and as individuals, as great or greater than the state supreme courts," she wrote in the *Court Review*, a publication of the American Judges Association. She urged readers to think of the City Court as a "court of first resort," paralleling the term *court of last resort*, which is the highest court of appeal within a legal jurisdiction. She saw too many unprepared lawyers, disrespectful defendants, unavailable arresting officers, and overworked court personnel, and the "courts of first resort" were all too often housed inadequately in seedy, roach-infested rooms. Since such courts constitute most people's only exposure to judicial proceedings, the legal community and the public needed to make the courts professional and dignified to foster respect for the judiciary as a whole. The newly minted judge also observed that an increasing number of judges in "courts of first resort" were "blacks, women, and other minorities just getting a toehold into the once exclusively all white male judiciary" and that many of the these highly qualified professionals "hope to serve on some of the higher courts one day."[22]

In 1988, after three years of full-time service on the traffic court, Leah Sears-Collins began to consider a new challenge. She heard about an upcoming vacancy on the Fulton County Superior Court, a court of general jurisdiction that handles both civil and criminal actions, but remained wary of the work that a campaign for an elected position would demand. A political campaign would require Leah to attend endless events, shake countless hands, and engage in hours of small talk, a draining prospect for an introvert who willed herself to function as an extrovert. In addition, the campaigning would take her away from her baby and toddler for long stretches of time. And somewhat uncharacteristically, she was afraid of failure. No woman had ever won a superior court judgeship in Fulton County, and no black woman had ever served on Georgia's highest trial court. Love Sears-Collins scoffed at her trepidation, pointing out,

"If you were a man, you wouldn't think about that. You'd run." She thought, "That's true. That is so true. *I will run!*" As she later reflected, "Women always talk themselves out of what they should be doing. Men gamble, take the risk, and get the high rewards. [Women] always figure out a way to wait." But not this time. Leah enlisted attorney Kevin Ross of Long Aldridge & Norman to serve as her campaign manager, and registered to run for the seat being vacated by the retirement of Judge John Langford.[23]

Leah's opponents were Ted Speaker, a white attorney, and Harris Bostic, a black attorney with deep roots in the African American community. "Harris Bostic was the pick of the black community," she recalled. "It had already been decided that it was his job, except no one informed me at the time." Leah belonged to what she described as an Atlanta cohort of well-educated, middle-class African American "affirmative action babies" who were viewed with suspicion when they started to take advantage of the opportunities for which the previous generation had fought. She was "suspect, and there was a big attempt initially to push [me] down." The attitude was, "'Who the hell are you? . . . We don't know you, you're from out of town.' It was sort of an Uncle Tom-ish 'You're not one of us!' thing." Once again, Leah was being perceived as "not black enough." In response, she doubled down, literally digging in her uncomfortable heels to hit the campaign trail: "I went everywhere. I wore conservative clothes and hard shoes, and I walked. Fulton County is long. We'd hit neighborhoods. I would walk them and knock on doors. I ruined my feet." Every Sunday, she attended three or four church services and pressed the flesh while Love, Rebecca Zimmerman, and other supporters worked the parking lots, putting flyers on cars. She spent hours each day researching issues on which she might be quizzed. She averaged less than four hours of sleep a night during the campaign season. The hard work paid off: Sears-Collins finished first in the August 9, 1988, election, earning 42.6 percent of the vote to Bostic's 34.9 percent and Speaker's 22.3 percent. But because no candidate had received a majority, a runoff election would be held.[24]

The campaign turned ugly. As a headline in the *Atlanta Journal-Constitution* announced, "Fulton Runoff for Judge Not a Staid Affair: Seen as Power Struggle in the Black Community." Bostic was supported by "Atlanta's old-guard black political establishment," including noted civil rights leader Ralph Abernathy, while Sears-Collins was backed by a "biracial coalition" that included not only

Mayor Young but also U.S. representative John Lewis, another esteemed veteran of the civil rights movement.[25]

Bostic focused on Sears-Collins's lack of experience as a trial attorney. Sears-Collins retorted that although she had not typically handled court cases in her law practice, she had presided over numerous jury trials during her traffic court tenure. Bostic also leveled less substantive charges at Sears-Collins, accusing her of incorrectly referring to herself as a judge after she had resigned her office to run for the superior court vacancy and of using City Court of Atlanta stationery for a campaign letter. More embarrassing for a former traffic court judge, Love Sears-Collins's car was impounded because he had accumulated numerous unpaid parking tickets and had let his tags expire. Leah Sears-Collins countered that Bostic had created the misleading impression that he was endorsed by another superior court judge and a Georgia Supreme Court justice. She also accused Bostic of having been sued for back taxes and debts thirty-one times over the preceding decade, resulting in judgments against him of more than nine thousand dollars, almost a third of which remained unpaid. Bostic blamed his financial issues on "poor clients who could not pay their legal bills, leaving him financially strapped at tax time, and a 1984 heart attack and quadruple bypass surgery that put him out of commission for two years."[26]

In the August 30, 1988, election, Leah Sears-Collins took 51 percent of the vote, becoming the first woman superior court judge in Fulton County and the first black woman superior court judge in Georgia. The chair of the Fulton County Commission, Michael Lomax, triumphantly proclaimed that her election to the $91,158-a-year seat made the bench "more representative of the community's racial and gender makeup, 'and thus, justice is a little more blind.'" Exultant and exhausted, Sears-Collins extended an olive branch to her opponent. "I want everyone to understand that Mr. Bostic was not *defeated*.... I happened to win. Mr. Bostic is a fine lawyer, and I look forward to having him practice in my court." She was disappointed by the tone of the race: "I was a little surprised when it got to be like a race for anything else. I thought it would be more courtly and a bit more dignified."[27]

On December 19, Sears-Collins took the oath of office at the Georgia Railroad Depot before a standing-room-only crowd. The oath was administered by Georgia Court of Appeals judge Dorothy Toth Beasley, who had been sworn in just four years earlier as the first woman to serve on an appellate court in Georgia. "I've spent the last 300 days running on all eight cylinders [and] I've never felt more aggressive and alive," Sears-Collins rejoiced, concluding her speech with "a prayer for humility, diligence, restraint and for sensitivity to the needs of 'others who are down and out and ask for mercy.'"[28]

Tom Sears rejoiced along with his daughter, proud that she would be ironing out the laws of the land instead of pillowcases. Continuing his own educational quest, in the spring of 1989 he added a degree in theology to his collection, which already included degrees in criminal justice, sociology, and law. He took the pulpit at the Midway First Presbyterian Church in Midway, Georgia, but in June, a routine physical revealed that he had kidney cancer. By November, he had been admitted to Savannah's Memorial Medical Center, struggling for breath. Leah made the eight-hour round-trip drive from Atlanta to Savannah as often as she could. When her father asked, "Have I done enough?" she replied, "Yes, you have. You've got a daughter who's on the Superior Court bench now. That's unfathomable! Just think about that! You've done a lot!" And she told him, "When you're ready, let go. I'll step in your shoes. I'll fight all your battles." He died on November 19.[29]

Leah Sears-Collins began to fulfill her promise to her father by pouring herself into her work, bringing her journalistic sensibilities and full-throttle style to a bench sorely in need of both. "Judges Say 'Briefs' No Longer Are," reported Atlanta's daily legal newspaper, describing a rash of out-of-control pleadings that further burdened the already-overloaded court system. Not only were "briefs" far too lengthy, the quality of writing had declined, causing judges to "grous[e] openly about the fat, sloppy paperwork." Sears-Collins tried to encourage and highlight pithy writing by showing staff members briefs and motions that impressed her. "I know that's a lawyer who likes his or her work well enough to give a little extra," she said. "It's okay to enjoy our jobs. . . . We should all take the time to discover the sheer fun and excitement that is everywhere in the practice of law." She saw tedious writing as an indicator that lawyers were not inspired by their work: "When I write an order, I like an order [that] I can really sink my teeth into and express my personality."[30]

She soon had an opportunity to provide a vivid example. While Sears-Collins had always enjoyed the give-and-take in the courtroom, one dispute went a bit too far, mutating into what she described as "virtual hand to hand combat between a landlord and his tenant over the nonpayment of rent." Leah consequently issued an "Order Temporarily Restraining Both Parties from Acting in an Uncivilized Manner" that enjoined each side from "threatening, intimidating, molesting, assaulting, scaring, frightening, alarming, chastising, harassing, vexing, attacking, insulting, cursing, damning, ravaging, abusing, slandering, mistreating, oppressing, victimizing, persecuting, manhandling, breaking in upon and otherwise causing himself to be a pain in the rear end to the other party, except as provided by the appropriate use of the legal process." The order was necessary, she maintained, "to keep the substantive legal issues raised in this case at a safe remove from the apparent desire of the parties to thrash each other good."[31]

Sears-Collins's sense of humor as well as her strong work ethic were necessary as she and her colleagues struggled to deal with a backlog of cases that had accumulated as a result of a 1988 lawsuit filed against the State Board of Elections by state representative Tyrone Brooks on behalf of the state's black voters. The class-action lawsuit alleged that Georgia's discriminatory method of electing judges resulted in a disproportionately low number of black judges and that the state had violated the Voting Rights Act of 1965 by failing to obtain preclearance for those methods through the U.S. Justice Department. The landmark Voting Rights Act of 1965 includes a provision that requires certain election law changes in "covered jurisdictions" to be approved by the Justice Department to ensure that those changes have no discriminatory purpose or effect.[32] Although Georgia was a "covered jurisdiction" under the act until 2013, the state had enacted eighty statutes regarding the election of superior court judges from 1964 to 1988 without seeking preclearance. In June 1988 the changes were submitted belatedly to the attorney general for clearance, but the addition of forty-eight judgeships and the redistricting of two circuits were not approved.

In response to the lawsuit, the state argued that the preclearance requirement did not apply to the judiciary, that the addition of a judgeship did not constitute a covered change, and that there was no potential for discrimination. A three-judge federal district court ruled against the state, noting that Georgia law precluded a system where all candidates competed against each other and judgeships were awarded to the highest vote-getters out of the field of candidates. Since a candidate had to run for a specific seat when more than one post existed in a circuit, a minority group could never elect a candidate without some majority-group votes. Therefore, the creation of new judge-ships under Georgia's rules meant that the potential for discrimination indeed existed. As a result, said the court, the state needed to obtain federal clearance to confirm that the voting procedures did not dilute minority voting power. The U.S. Supreme Court affirmed the decision, giving a "powerful weapon to the lawyers who [were] trying to integrate the nation's primarily white, elected state judiciary."[33]

No elections could be held to fill the expiring terms until the Justice Department acted. And even though judges were allowed to remain in their posts until a new electoral scheme was cleared and implemented, a court order prevented the governor from filling any vacancies. That year, Fulton County was operating four judges short of the fourteen authorized by the General Assembly, and their caseload was rising at an alarming rate—more than 20 percent between 1988 and 1989. The sitting judges were "bailing water," according to Sears-Collins, who was working overtime and on weekends just to keep up. Still, she thought "it was wonderful!" She loved the attorneys who appeared before her in court "because they were all characters. [I would ask] 'What do you have for me today?' And they always had something. It's a great job for me, halfway between academia and being right in the trenches. You can't beat it."[34]

Domestic relations cases constituted about one-third of Sears-Collins's caseload. Two of those cases made national news and illustrated her evolving dedication to preserving intact families. In the first case, Jeffrey Vogel had been given up for adoption by his unmarried parents, eighteen-year-old David and seventeen-year-old Heather, one day after he was born on February 4, 1991. When the couple relinquished their rights to their child, the agency, Friends of Children, told them that they had ten days, starting February 6, to change their minds. Since February 16 was a Saturday, David and Heather assumed that the deadline would move to the next business day, Monday, February 18. David and Heather subsequently reconsidered and decided to get married and keep their son. They made an appointment to see the baby on February 13, and David took that day off from his job as the manager of a fast-food restaurant. However, that afternoon their caseworker called to say that the baby had a doc-tor's appointment and that the visit had to be postponed until February 18. When David and Heather arrived to reclaim their child, the agency informed them that they were three days too late: the deadline had been midnight on February 15. Though the child had not yet been placed with an adoptive family, the agency refused to return him to David and Heather.

The Vogels filed suit in Fulton County to get their child back. Judge Sears-Collins ordered the adoption agency to keep the baby in foster care and gave attorneys ten days to submit further briefs. She promised that her ruling would come quickly so that the baby would not remain in legal limbo. "This isn't a used-car transaction," she reminded the parties. "This is a human being." But this was a human being with monetary value: a healthy white infant would net the adoption agency approximately twenty-five thousand dollars. "The market for babies is so lucrative and unregulated in Georgia that the adoption of healthy white infants now borders on baby selling," reported the *Atlanta Constitution*. "Desperate couples and single adults wait up to six years to adopt a child. If they go through a private agency, they'll pay as much as $17,000 for a foreign infant—$25,000 'plus some incidentals' for a healthy white one from Friends of Children."[35]

Sears-Collins found that the couple had missed the contractual deadline for withdrawing their surrender. However, the surrender could be legally voided upon a finding of "good and sufficient cause." She found it, blasting what she saw as "an adoption agency seeking finality in order to make, what appears to be, a quick and handsome profit from the placement of a child in an adoptive home." Sears-Collins ruled that the couple had not fully comprehended the deadline, which the agency should have made clear. In addition, she found that David Vogel had been coerced into signing an adoption consent form when Friends of Children threatened to seek reimbursement for the thirteen hundred dollars that the agency had paid for the mother's rent, food, and medical expenses. He had "executed his consent at a time when he had no one to turn to for legal advice . . . and was suffering under tremendous emotional strain." The judge noted that there were no prospective adoptive parents to consider and accused the agency of impairing the couple's attempts to see their child before the revocation deadline had passed. And with that, in the "emotionally charged courtroom setting," the blue-eyed, dark-haired baby, now 2 ½ months old, was placed in his parents' arms.[36]

The second case began shortly after the Vogel case was resolved. A thirteen-year-old girl known as Jane Doe was admitted to the Scottish Rite Children's

Medical Center and diagnosed with an irreversible, degenerative neurological disorder that had destroyed most of her brain. She fluctuated between stupor and coma, and the physicians caring for her declared that she had no chance of "meaningful recovery" and that the only feeling she could experience was pain. The hospital discussed the possibility of terminating the child's life support with her parents: her mother, "Susan Doe" backed deescalation of life support and a "do not resuscitate" (DNR) order, but her father, "John Doe," opposed both courses of action for religious reasons. The girl's mother asked to have the situation presented to Scottish Rite's Bioethics Committee, which recommended that the hospital support Susan Doe's wishes.

Four months after Jane Doe was admitted, the hospital filed suit, asking the court to declare what it should do when parents disagreed about the appropriate course of medical treatment for their child. Susan Doe then began to vacillate, backing off from her opinion that life support should be deescalated but still supporting a DNR order. During two days of "wrenching and tearful testimony," one of Jane Doe's physicians testified that hospital personnel caring for the girl "felt they were torturing the child with the aggressive treatments needed to keep her alive." "With patients who have any hope of a meaningful recovery we tolerate this, but without that hope it is abuse," he said. Other medical workers testified of having nightmares about what they were forcing the child to endure. They also testified that they believed that Jane Doe's mother was just as emotionally fatigued and that she wanted her daughter to die in peace but was afraid of her husband's anger and blame.[37]

The hospital, the parents, and the nation waited for Sears-Collins's decision. As the *New York Times* pointed out, "Medical ethicists and partisans in the right-to-die debates were hard-pressed to identify another case that combined so many troubling elements. Not only did it involve a disagreement among family members revolving around religious beliefs, it involved a dispute between a hospital and a parent over what was futile and hopeless. The case also involved an assertion by doctors that their life-sustaining efforts could become so painful as to be abusive. And it featured an attempt to displace parental judgment even though the parents were not deemed neglectful or acting against the child's best interest."[38]

Leah Sears-Collins found herself consulting her old college textbooks on human development to ponder "the broader philosophical and religious issues, such as how do we as human beings live? What is life all about?" Finally, she decided to visit the girl. When she entered the child's room, she saw a picture of a sunrise drawn by the girl's younger sister and inscribed, "Good Morning, Sunshine." "What are her chances of survival?" the judge asked, gazing at the little blond girl with tubes running into her stomach, throat, and nose. Her physician answered that there would be "no more good mornings for his patient." With constant intensive care, she could linger, in pain, for approximately a year.[39]

Sears-Collins, who often prioritized relationships when making a decision, woke up the next morning thinking, "I can't figure out her condition. I don't know where she is on this plane . . . between life and death. But her parents are split. . . . If I remove her from life support, she will die within a few hours, and they will separate and divorce. And they have other kids. And the other kids will suffer. Because you can't kill a child and keep the family together." She ordered Scottish Rite Children's Hospital not to remove the child's respirator unless both parents agreed: "This court finds that if either parent, in the exercise of his or her rights with regard to the welfare of Jane Doe, makes the decision to continue Jane Doe's life, as the father has in this case, that decision must be respected." The deescalation of treatment would "impinge upon the father's freedom of religion" and was "antithetical to our scheme of ordered liberty and to our respect for the autonomy of the individual and the family for a third party to make decisions regarding an individual's quality of life. It is for the patient or, in the case of a child, her parents to decide such issues." Then she ordered the attorney general to appeal her decision to the Supreme Court of Georgia to provide guidelines for future cases.[40]

"Judge Sears-Collins seems to hold that parents have an absolute right to make decisions about the medical treatment of their children, barring evidence of severe neglect, abuse or endangerment," reported the *Atlanta Constitution*. "Are there no circumstances when the state or third parties such as hospitals are justified in overruling the parents? Can the state interest in allocating scarce medical resources ever outweigh a particular family's desire to keep a loved one in some state of existence? The constitutional right to freely exercise one's religion is not absolute. It must be weighed against other rights and interests. Would it make a difference if Jane Doe were in a persistently vegetative state rather than alternating between stupor and coma? Should a parent's faith in miraculous healing be allowed to determine hospital policy? The conundrums of life and death posed by today's medical technology do not allow for simple, absolute answers."[41]

Colorful Georgia defense attorney Bobby Lee Cook wrote to Leah Sears-Collins, "Your decision was a very scholarly one on a very difficult subject and which touched all the bases, morally and legally. . . . Most recently I had the same problem where I represented the parents who took the same position as the parents in your case but the matter was resolved without a hearing. . . . I have not had the pleasure of meeting you or knowing you but, without an attempt at judicial flattery, a talent on the bench such as yours should not go unnoticed."[42]

Jane Doe died within a week, surrounded by her family. Nine months later, six of the seven justices on the Supreme Court of Georgia affirmed the judgment. The court pointed out that since both parents opposed deescalation of treatment at the time of the hearing, the trial court was correct to enjoin the hospital from deescalating treatment. As for the DNR order, the court determined that one parent could revoke consent. "The result is as follows: One parent may consent. If there is no second parent, if the other parent is not present, or if the other parent simply prefers not to participate in the decision, the consent of one parent to a DNR order is legally sufficient under the statute. However, if there is a second custodial parent who disagrees with the decision to forego cardiopulmonary resuscitation, the second parent may revoke consent. . . . We reject the argument that only the parent who has given consent may effectively revoke consent. Where two parents have legal custody of a child, each parent shares equal decision-making responsibility for that child. If consent to a DNR order is revoked . . . , the hospital must follow the statutory presumption that every patient is presumed to consent to resuscitation. Thus, because the father revoked consent, the trial court correctly determined the hospital could not enter a DNR order."[43]

The seventh justice—and only woman on the Supreme Court of Georgia—was disqualified from hearing the appeal of the Jane Doe ruling. That justice was Leah Sears-Collins.

Leah Sears in pigtails, her *Sound of Music* look (with Onnye).
Courtesy of Leah Ward Sears.

Tommy, Leah, and Michael Sears. Onnye kept her children
well groomed and well dressed to command respect.
Courtesy of Haskell Sears Ward.

Leah Sears was one of three
black Girl Scouts in her troop.
Courtesy of Leah Ward Sears.

Leah Sears in her award-filled office next to
Leroy Campbell's giclée, *Good Hair*, December
2015. Courtesy of Leah Ward Sears and
Leroy Campbell.

Leah Sears-Collins during her tenure as a traffic
court judge on the City Court of Atlanta,
ca. 1985. Courtesy of Leah Ward Sears.

Haskell Ward in Uganda, 1964. Courtesy of Haskell Sears Ward.

Haskell Sears Ward and Leah Ward Sears
on their wedding day, April 18, 1999.
Courtesy of Susan J. Ross.

Campaign photo of Leah Ward Sears in front of a photo
of her father, Lieutenant Colonel Tom Sears, 2004.
Courtesy of Rebecca Zimmerman.

Leah Ward Sears is sworn in as the first black woman chief justice of a
state high court, June 28, 2005. *L to R*: Leah, Haskell Sears Ward,
Addison Sears-Collins, Onnye Sears, Brennan Sears-Collins, and former
U.N. ambassador Andrew Young. Courtesy of Haskell Sears Ward.

U.S. Supreme Court justice Clarence Thomas,
Georgia chief justice Leah Ward Sears, and former
U.N. ambassador Andrew Young at Leah Ward Sears's
investiture as chief justice, June 28, 2005.
Courtesy of Haskell Sears Ward.

Fiat Justitia Ruat Caelum (Let justice be done though the heavens fall): The Supreme Court of Georgia, 2005. *Back row, L to R*: Justices P. Harris Hines, George H. Carley, Hugh P. Thompson, and Harold Melton. *Front row, L to R*: Presiding Justice Carol W. Hunstein, Chief Justice Leah Ward Sears, Justice Robert Benham. Courtesy of the Supreme Court of Georgia.

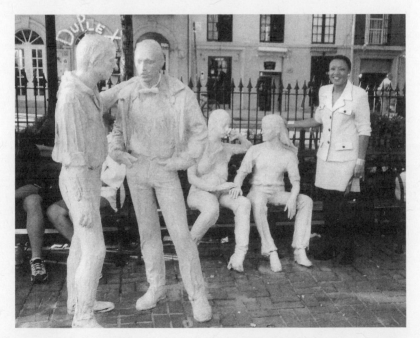

Leah Ward Sears in New York City's Christopher Park next to George Segal's sculpture, *Gay Liberation*, which commemorates the events at the Stonewall Inn. Courtesy of Haskell Sears Ward.

Leah Sears-Collins celebrates becoming Georgia's first black woman superior court judge, 1988. *L to R*: Atlanta mayor Andrew Young, Leah Sears-Collins, U.S. representative John Lewis, and Fulton County Commission chair Michael Lomax. Courtesy of Leah Ward Sears.

Leah Sears-Collins and Maynard Jackson, 1988. Courtesy of Leah Ward Sears.

CHAPTER 4

The Year of the Woman

Diversity on the bench is critical. As practitioners, you need judges
who "get it!" We need judges who understand what discrimination feels like.
We need judges who understand what inequality feels like. We need judges
who understand the subtleties of unfair treatment and who are
willing to call it out when they see it!
—Debbie Wasserman Schultz

It was 1992. Betty Daniels heard muffled sobbing coming from behind the closed door, followed by, "I won't let you down. Thank you so much, Governor!" Concerned, Daniels cracked open the door and peeked inside her boss's office. "Supreme Court!" Leah Sears-Collins mouthed, covering up the mouthpiece on the phone. Seconds later, Sears-Collins hung up and burst through the door. "Supreme Court!" she cried. Her office erupted in a cacophony of joyful screams. This meant that Daniels would have to move again, but she couldn't say she minded.

Betty was working at Long Aldridge & Norman for Kevin Ross, manager of Sears-Collins's campaign for the superior court judgeship, when the two women were introduced a few years earlier. "Don't tell me you're Colonel Sears's daughter!" exclaimed Betty. She had lived in Savannah and had worked with Tom Sears on a program to help underprivileged high school students get to college. Moreover, Betty had cousins who lived just a few houses away from the Sears family, and she had often seen Leah there.

In 1988, Ross was planning to leave the firm to run the Atlanta mayoral campaign of Maynard Jackson, Young's predecessor in the Atlanta mayor's office and the first African American to hold that post. With Young prohibited from seeking a third consecutive term, Jackson had decided to make a bid to return to the office in 1989. Ross encouraged Daniels to contact Sears-Collins about becoming her administrative assistant. When Daniels hesitated, Ross told her, "You have an opportunity to work for a judge. You can't stay here at this law firm. That's just not a good choice." Over lunch, Daniels and Sears-Collins discussed the options, and then Daniels cut to the chase: "Now that we've talked—are you going to hire me or not? Because you already know whether you're going to hire me or not." Sears-Collins replied, "I like your nerve. Yes, I will hire you." But then Daniels got cold feet and started avoiding Sears-Collins's attempts to finalize the details. The judge eventually left Daniels a message: "There is another woman I'd like to hire. If you don't want the job, let me know." Daniels decided that she was in. She later learned that there was no other woman, but by that point, Sears-Collins had gotten what she wanted.[1]

Sears-Collins's journey to the Supreme Court of Georgia began when presiding justice George T. Smith, the only person to win contested elections in all three branches of state government, reluctantly retired from the bench in 1991. Smith, a former lieutenant governor and Speaker of the Georgia House of Representatives, had joined the court in 1981. Georgia law mandated that justices retire from the court at age seventy, but in 1986, when Smith reached that age, the legislature revised the law to permit him to remain. Five years later, however, Smith bumped into the state law that required appellate court judges (that is, those sitting on either the Supreme Court or the Court of Appeals) to resign by age seventy-five or forfeit their pensions. Smith had sued to overturn the law but lost, blaming Governor Zell Miller, who had vetoed legislation that would have again raised the mandatory retirement age: "It was pure old unadulterated politics," claimed Smith, "designed to create a vacancy and give Mr. Miller an opportunity to appoint his own man."[2]

Or woman. Miller wanted to boost the diversity of the court, on which no woman and only one African American, current justice Robert Benham, had ever served. Smith's legal defeat actually meant that Miller could appoint two appellate court judges, since the presiding judge of the Court of Appeals, Harold Banke, a coplaintiff in the lawsuit, had also reached age seventy-five.

Georgia's Court of Appeals is an intermediate appellate court; sitting in panels of three, it hears appeals in all cases where exclusive or general jurisdiction is not reserved to the Supreme Court. Twelve judges served on the Court of Appeals when Banke retired, though that number increased to fifteen in 2016. The Supreme Court, Georgia's highest court, hears cases decided in the lower appellate court or in one of the trial courts. In some instances, litigants have a right to a direct appeal; others require litigants to ask the Supreme Court to take their cases. If a losing litigant files a petition for writ of certiorari, the Supreme Court has the discretion to grant or deny the petition. The court grants certiorari when the justices believe that a case raises an issue of great concern or importance to the public. The Georgia Supreme Court has exclusive appellate jurisdiction in cases involving construction of the Georgia Constitution and the U.S. Constitution, and decisions may be appealed to the U.S. Supreme Court only if they involve the interpretation of the U.S. Constitution or federal laws. Thus, while the U.S. Supreme Court is the final arbiter of federal constitutional questions, the Georgia Supreme Court is the final arbiter of state laws and state constitutional questions.

The Georgia Supreme Court sits for three terms each year, and according to the state constitution, the court's decisions must be rendered within two terms. That, combined with the appeals the court is required by law to hear, makes it one of the busiest appellate courts in the country. The court's docket averages two thousand cases per year, and the justices issue written opinions in more than four hundred cases annually.[3]

Leah Sears-Collins was eager to join one of the two appellate courts. She had recently gotten a taste of serving on an appellate court, and she was hooked. Justice Robert Benham had gotten Sears-Collins's name placed on the designated judges list, and she was asked to step in when Chief Justice Clarke was unable to serve. "That's when it hit her," remembered Daniels. "She said: 'I want to do this. This is *beautiful*.'" The appellate court suited Sears-Collins's personality. She relished reading, writing, and analytical thinking, and she was already known for crafting opinions "with the look and feel of something emanating from the higher bench."[4]

The Judicial Nominating Commission, which screens candidates for judgeships, had called for nominations for the two positions. The commission's questionnaires had to be returned by January 31, 1992, less than a month after the call for nominations. Each day after court, Sears-Collins and Daniels worked on refining her answers. Believing that "her best writing as a trial judge came in cases of parental anguish," she listed the Vogel and Jane Doe cases as two of her most significant rulings.[5]

The commission received thirty-eight nominations for the seat on the Supreme Court, approximately half of them (including Sears-Collins's) from the nominees themselves. Thirty-three people submitted the required paperwork, and the Judicial Nominating Commission reviewed the applications and winnowed the list down to ten finalists, among them seven women. Other names on the impressive list included Court of Appeals judge Dorothy Toth Beasley, the first woman to serve on a Georgia appellate court, and DeKalb County Superior Court judge Carol W. Hunstein, who had served as a designated judge on the Georgia Supreme Court in the Smith case.[6]

The governor would interview the candidates in his office during the week of February 10. Everyone expected him to appoint a woman to the Supreme Court, and Sears-Collins was not the only African American woman on the list. How could she make herself stand out? Once again, she had no natural allies: "I didn't come out of the black caucus; I wasn't their choice. I wasn't the women's choice, because the women's choice would have been a judge who had been around a long time. I was younger than [the others] were." And that, she decided, was what she had to offer: her youth. The thirty-six-year-old judge compiled a list of youthful game-changers whom she could cite as impressive examples.[7]

On the day of her interview, Sears-Collins walked into the room and fixed her eyes on the fifty-nine-year-old ex-marine. For some reason, his cowboy boots put her at ease. She liked the fact that Miller was unconventional, and she identified with his independent streak. They discussed the Brooks litigation regarding Georgia's method of choosing judges and her goals for the future while he took copious notes on a yellow legal pad. Then, Sears tackled the subject of her youth: "You are probably wondering about my age," she began. "I know I'm only thirty-six. But Richard Russell was only thirty-five when he went to the U.S. Senate. Thomas Jefferson was only thirty-three when he wrote the Declaration of Independence. My father was only twenty-three when he went off to fight the Korean War. I am a product of the post-civil-rights and post–Vietnam War era, and I could add a very different dimension to the court.

Youth has no place at the table right now, and everyone on the court doesn't have to be an old man." Miller was delighted. Sears's bench experience had impressed him, and she had indeed differentiated herself from the other nominees. "That woman has spunk!" he reportedly told Cynthia Wright, his chief legal counsel.[8]

On February 17, Leah and Love Sears-Collins were out at lunch when the governor's assistant called. "Can I have her return your call?" Betty asked. "No. We'll call her." As soon as Sears-Collins returned, the phone rang again. She at first thought that Miller was giving her a courtesy call to tell her she had not been selected. When she realized that he was calling with good news, she believed that she was being offered the vacancy on the Court of Appeals. When she finally understood what was happening, she was floored. The Supreme Court! She was going to become the first woman on Georgia's highest court and just the second African American woman on any such court in any state. Miller relished the hoopla that followed his surprise appointment, and he responded to critics with the same argument that Sears-Collins had used: "I remind them that Richard Russell had already served as governor of Georgia and moved to the United States Senate at her age." He added that he had chosen Sears-Collins "because she possesses in abundance the qualities an outstanding jurist should have: intellect, temperament, and energy" and that he believed "she has the potential to become one of the nation's most brilliant and sensitive jurists."[9]

The Georgia Council for Children's Rights was thrilled. At the superior court, Sears-Collins had established a mediation program for domestic relations cases, which accounted for about one-third of her caseload. Prior to meeting with a mediation coordinator, she required litigants to watch a videotape, *Don't Forget the Children*, that stressed the impact of custody battles on all involved parties. Almost all of her domestic relations cases settled. The council had recently featured Sears-Collins in its publication, *Voices for Children*, for her approach to family and children law and for the past two years had listed her among its top ten Georgia judges.[10]

Atlanta's mayor was also over the moon. "Maynard Jackson couldn't stop calling me," said Sears-Collins. "And I didn't have the time to get back. He kept calling me, saying, 'I'm proud! I'm proud! I'm proud! I'm amazed!'" Television cameras made their way to the Sears-Collins home in Ansley Park, where a reporter had five-year-old Brennan turn a cartwheel as a visual meta-phor for the family's festive mood. Addison, eight years old, had a more real-istic idea of what his mother's new job was going to entail: "I think it's a lot of hard work," he observed with a grin. Coretta Scott King wrote to congrat-ulate Sears-Collins, declaring the appointment "another shared triumph for the cause of progressive social change and equal opportunity." Chief Justice Harold Clarke noted with approval that "his new colleague [was] younger than his older daughter," which gave her added value to the court because "if you just had seven people all the same age who lived through the same expe-riences and all had the same interests, then you might as well just have one person on the bench." But the euphoria was not universal. Some observers were perplexed by the governor's unusual choice and asked her, "Who the hell are you? We have labored for years, and then he picks *you*? Why you?" She recalled, "A lot of people, including many blacks from the establishment, weren't looking to me to be the pick. I was Miller's pick. I wasn't *anybody* else's pick! I think that Miller likes to do the unpredictable. And I was cer-tainly an unpredictable pick." One man even suggested that she had gotten the appointment by sleeping with the governor.[11]

Hundreds of friends, family, and well-wishers crammed into the state senate chambers on March 6 to witness Sears-Collins's swearing-in. "The justices who now sit on the bench of the Georgia Supreme Court are all excellent judges, and we are very fortunate to have them there. But they are all of the same gender, and the same generation—my gender and my generation," remarked Miller. "So I did approach this appointment with an eye on diversity, looking to enrich our highest court with a fresh perspective. Leah Sears-Collins was not the only woman in the candidate group—there were six others. Nor was she the only minority candidate or the only candidate who could bring in the perspective of a younger generation. But, she combined all three of these traits, of course, and even more importantly, she had a proven level of excellence on the bench.... I am very proud to be the Governor to appoint and swear her in as a justice on the Supreme Court of the State of Georgia." Sears-Collins got a standing ovation when she approached the podium. She thanked Miller for appointing her as the first woman justice. "I have attained in my life what was, when I was born, an unattainable goal," she said. State representative Tyrone Brooks agreed, proclaiming it "a great day for Georgia" and adding that he had never dreamed that a black female would sit on the Georgia Supreme Court in his lifetime. Sears-Collins also thanked her children for their patience and for their "willingness, even eagerness, to have a few more dinners catered from Dominos Pizza."[12]

Sears-Collins was aware that hard work and sacrifice would follow the celebration. "There's always a heavier burden, I think, for a woman or a black or—my gosh—a black woman who is thirty-six years old to make it clear that you are here on your own merits and to become respected on your own merits," she acknowledged. Shortly after she joined the court, Justice Richard Bell informed her that she was too young to be there after he referred to "the War" and she didn't know whether he was referring to World War II or the Vietnam War. So to prove her worth, she began each day at 5:30 in the morning, reading briefs, triple-checking facts, rehearsing her arguments, and having her staff critique her performance so she could improve. She wore conservative clothes. As noted law professor Deborah L. Rhode, a contemporary of Sears-Collins's, has noted, affirmative action for women and minorities required them "to prove that they 'deserved' the positions at issue and were not simply the beneficiaries of preferential treatment. Hard work, extended hours, and exceptional competence were the strategies of choice, but a sense of humor could be useful as well." Sears embraced all of these strategies.[13]

She eventually became more comfortable with her fellow jurists when Justice Charles Weltner, sensing her uneasiness over how to address her much older male colleagues, pulled her aside and advised her, "Call me Charlie," and Justice Willis Hunt began to quiet the other justices during meetings so that her voice could be heard. "You may not think the way we do," Hunt told her, "but I love the way you write, and I'm not just blowing smoke up your skirt!"[14]

Sears-Collins's first appearance in court began with a brief moment of embarrassment when her colleagues remained standing as she sat down with the first rap of the gavel instead of the second, as was their custom. Despite that hiccup, she dived right into the process and within months had earned a reputation as one of the court's most dedicated workers. "She comes to work early, stays late, is there on weekends, and takes piles of work home," wrote one reporter who interviewed her alone in her office while she was plowing through a stack of briefs on July 3, not only a national holiday but also her sixteenth wedding anniversary. And although she claimed that her age had more impact on her perspective than did her gender or her race, all three characteristics came into play.[15]

The issue of equity and race moved to the top of national agenda on April 29, 1992, less than eight weeks after Sears-Collins took office, when prosecutors failed to win the convictions of four Los Angeles policemen on criminal assault charges stemming from the beating of African American motorist Rodney King. On March 3, 1991, King had been stopped by officers after a high-speed car chase and then severely beaten. The assault on King was caught on video and shown on television, where millions of viewers were horrified by what appeared to be unrestrained police brutality against an unarmed man suspected of a nonviolent offense. Despite the video evidence, a jury that did not include any blacks acquitted three officers, and a mistrial was declared for the other. The verdict sparked an explosion of violence in Los Angeles and several other cities. Revolted by a system they saw as structurally skewed against African Americans, rioters erupted in rage, engaging in several days of looting, arson, and homicide. Kasim Reed, at the time a twenty-two-year-old Howard University graduate who had just run for the Fulton County Commission and later the mayor of Atlanta, described the King beating and the outcome of the trial as illustrating the type of harassment black males routinely endured. During his campaign, Reed said, white police officers had harassed him three times while he was putting up signs and canvassing neighborhoods: "I don't exploit race. But I know when fairness has been breached." On May 1, Atlanta University Center students and riot police traded tear gas, bricks, and stones, with other incidents of violence occurring in smaller Georgia cities as well. The rioting caused Leah Sears Collins to realize that "there is a perception among many that the judicial system is not fair."[16]

Barely a month after the King verdict, the Georgia Supreme Court accepted the recommendation of the Judicial Qualifications Commission that the chief magistrate of Upson County, Vivian Hammock, receive a thirty-day suspension as punishment for her treatment of a black associate magistrate she had been forced to hire as a result of a federal suit. Judge William Hughley, a twenty-nine-year-old former math teacher, was made to work from eight in the evening until eight in the morning, Monday through Saturday, first in a storage room and later out of the trunk of his car when Hammock banned him from the courthouse. While Sears-Collins's colleagues were appalled and found

Hammock's actions "reprehensible . . . and indefensible from either a moral or legal standpoint," the situation hit closer to home for Sears-Collins, who wrote an indignant concurring opinion: "No one called upon to judge the citizens of Georgia should ever be allowed to exercise power in such a manner as to scorn and hold up to contempt another because he is of a different race. It is unnatural, arrogant, indecent, unfair, oppressive and repulsive to the American system of justice, and it cannot be tolerated. When a judge, who has sworn to administer justice instead undermines it, she is repudiating her sworn duty to the citizens of this state and, therefore, ought herself to be repudiated."[17]

The following year, Sears-Collins and Robert Benham, whose great-great grandparents had been slaves, were the only two justices who sided with the defendant in a case where "race-based innuendo and subtle stereotyping [were] used to exclude people of color" from a jury in a death penalty case involving African American defendant Rodney Lingo. During jury selection, both the prosecutor and the defense counsel may challenge an unlimited number of prospective jurors for a lack of impartiality. The parties also have a limited number of peremptory strikes, which allow prospective jurors to be removed without showing cause. In 1986, however, the U.S. Supreme Court ruled in *Batson v. Kentucky* that it is unconstitutional to use peremptory challenges to exclude jurors because of their race. A peremptory strike may be challenged by showing a "prima facie" (Latin for "at first view") case for discrimination— that is, enough evidence to support the claim. If the court finds that a peremptory strike appears racially discriminatory, the opposing party must provide a neutral explanation for striking the juror. This explanation, in turn, can be overcome if the challenger can show that the racially neutral reason was just a pretext for deliberate discrimination. This process creates a high legal hurdle: it is fairly easy to provide a facially neutral explanation for striking a juror and difficult to prove deliberate discrimination.[18]

The white members of the Georgia Supreme Court found a very strong inference of racial discrimination in the *Lingo* case but accepted as racially neutral the prosecutor's reasons for exercising his peremptory strikes against prospective black jurors, though the same reasons were not used to strike white jurors. The court opined that "it cannot be *presumed* that a reason applied to one juror, of one race, but not applied to another juror, of another race, is racially motivated." Sears-Collins and Benham took a different view: "When it comes to grappling with racial issues in the criminal justice system today, often white Americans find one reality while African-Americans see another," Sears-Collins wrote in her dissent. This observation remains applicable today.

> The prosecutor explained that one potential black juror was struck because: he was "touchy" about one of the prosecutor's first questions and "hostile from there on"; he had previously testified in a trial as a character witness; and had taken some criminal justice classes. [The] record reveals that other than being initially surprised by the prosecutor's knowledge of information the juror had provided on his juror questionnaire, the juror showed no indication of being "hostile" towards the prosecutor. . . . I still cannot believe that a white juror who gave exactly the same responses to the voir dire questions that this juror gave would have been labeled "hostile" and "belligerent." The hostility and belligerence found so readily by the prosecutor and the trial judge from this juror's one response evoke stereotypical images of the angry black man, who, at the slightest provocation and at even the faintest appearance of challenging the status quo will be tagged "hostile" or "belligerent." . . . [T]he prosecutor accepted without complaint a white juror who had previously testified in a trial as a character witness. . . . [E]ven assuming that the fact that the juror had taken some criminal justice classes was a non-racially motivated reason for striking this juror, both the prosecutor's application of the racial stereotype of the "hostile black male" and his failure to neutrally apply his other reason for striking this juror force me to conclude that improper racial motives played a role in the prosecutor's striking the juror. . . . We stand at the edge of the 21st century and Black people in this country are still not free from insidious racial discrimination such as that manifested in this case. The constitutions of the United States and of Georgia demand the *total, uncompromising* racial neutrality of the jury selection process to ensure every American's right to fully participate, and Rodney Dwayne Lingo did not receive that neutrality. My candor in this dissent may lead some to believe that I am "hostile." I am not. I am, however, fully committed to the promise of the U.S. and Georgia Constitutions to afford their rights and privileges fully to all citizens.[19]

Judge Charles Mikell, a member of the Georgia Supreme Court Commission on Racial and Ethnic Bias in the Court System, wrote to Sears-Collins to express his respect for her dissent: "Our commission has heard repeated complaints in public hearings about abuse of peremptory strikes, especially in death penalty cases. The *Lingo* case illustrates the obvious severity of the problem and the difficulties of the continuing debate about how to handle *Batson* objections at the trial and appellate levels."[20]

―――――

Sears-Collins's status as the only woman on the court with young children also influenced her perception of the issues and their legal ramifications and at times made a difference to the court as a whole. When the court received the 1992 appeal of a lower-court decision to allow police officers to use the consent of a ten-year-old child to search his parents' home, Sears-Collins could easily picture herself and her nine-year-old in that situation. She was initially the only justice who thought the court should hear the case, "horrified by what the police had done here, turning this child against his parents." She convinced her colleagues of the impact the case could have on families; consequently, the other six justices agreed to hear the case. When they did, they unanimously agreed with her that the boy's consent was not valid. In finding that the officers violated the parents' Fourth Amendment right to privacy in their home, Sears-Collins wrote,

> The younger a child the less likely that he or she can be said to have the minimal discretion required to validly consent to a search, much less waive important constitutional rights. Judicial vigilance is especially merited when, as here, the child is quite young. Most ten-year-old children are incapable of understanding and waiving their own rights, much less those of their parents. . . . [I]t appears to us that [the child] believed that by calling the police and reporting that his parents had drugs in the house he would achieve familial harmony, not disharmony, disruption, and the burden of the state's enforcement powers. . . . This child simply did not know or completely understand what the consequences of his consent would be. . . . Our decision is intended to imply no criticism of [the child] or of the police, and certainly no praise for the appellant. By this opinion we simply acknowledge the right of privacy in one's home, and, under the facts present, we refuse to entrust that precious right to the judgment of the ten-year-old child in this case.

The following year, Sears-Collins cited the case as "a prime example of why we need diversity in the judiciary. She continued, "We need people of all backgrounds, all ages, and differing life experiences. At the same time, we need judges who are open-minded and willing to listen to what their fellow judges have to say."[21]

Sears-Collins's perspective molded the court's opinions in other ways as well, as when she prevented the court from issuing an opinion with language she considered unnecessary and outdated. She objected to a draft opinion by Justice Benham that included the sentence, "The holding comports with reasoning set forth by our brethren over a century ago in *Silvey v. State*," and declared her intention to issue a concurring opinion if the language was not changed:

> This court . . . has gone to great lengths and much expense to uncover and dis-
> courage gender bias in the court system, and our legislature has taken pains
> to rid Georgia's statutes of gender specific language where it is not necessary.
> Although I recognize that the Georgia Supreme Court of 1889 was all male,
> I believe that the majority's embrace of the unnecessary term "our brethren"
> ("brethren" is the plural of "brother") in reference to that court, when many
> other terms would have been suitable, diminishes these very important goals,
> which this Court should lead the effort to attain.

Once again, the other justices were persuaded, and the revised—and unani-mous—opinion read, "The holding comports with reasoning set forth by this court over a century ago in *Silvey v. State*."[22]

Sears-Collins's presence on the bench at times proved an embarrassing stumbling block for lawyers practicing before the court. Sears-Collins rebuked one attorney after he used the phrase "Gentlemen of the court" more than half a dozen times, oblivious to the inappropriateness of his words. Some female lawyers, however, were inspired by the sight of a woman Supreme Court jus-tice. The co-chair of the State Bar of Georgia's Committee on Women's and Minority Affairs became almost tearful when she walked into the court and saw Sears-Collins sitting with the other justices.[23]

———

The move to Georgia's highest court was literally costly for Sears-Collins: her $92,778 salary as a Supreme Court justice was about 10 percent less than she received at the superior court. The pay cut was the first thing she mentioned on a lighthearted "Best of a Supreme" list she gave to *Creative Loafing*, an alternative weekly newspaper: "You pay fewer taxes because you make about $10,000 less than you did as a lower-level judge." More significantly, she immediately had to begin campaigning to retain her seat. In Georgia, although the governor can appoint justices to fill interim vacancies on the Supreme Court, appointees must win an election to remain in office. Nonpartisan judicial elections for appellate court judges are held on Georgia's primary date, which in 1992 was July 21. Moreover, because the contest would be a statewide election, Sears-Collins would have to run and win in counties that had never elected a black official. She would have to "depend on the good ol' boy network to deliver for her in areas where the homeboy network" could not.[24]

The 1992 judicial elections were expected to be the last in which Georgia voters would choose their trial and appellate court judges. Governor Miller had sought to settle the four-year-old litigation regarding racial diversity on the bench by having the state transition to the Missouri Plan (also known as merit selection). Under the plan, the governor would appoint justices from a list of candidates submitted by the Judicial Nominating Commission. The appointee would then face a nonpartisan, uncontested retention election every four years. Miller had agreed to have at least twenty-five black superior court judges sitting on the bench by the end of 1994 and to appoint five additional blacks to either superior or state courts. At the time, Georgia had 9 African Americans among its 156 superior court judges, a disproportionately small number in a state where 27 percent of the population was black. Leah Sears-Collins, however, was not interested in being perceived as having won a seat on the state's highest court because of her race or gender. "I've worked my butt off," she declared.[25]

Though campaigning made Sears-Collins uncomfortable and took time away from her work on the court, it was necessary if she were to reach her goal of avoiding going "down in history as the judge with the shortest term on the bench." In 1990, she had offered a workshop, "You Be the Judge," in which she taught other women and minorities the networking, fund-raising, and publicity skills that they would need to conduct a judicial campaign. Now she had to apply those skills herself. Her opponent, Clayton Superior Court judge Stephen Boswell, had announced his candidacy before Sears-Collins's appointment, and he fit the profile of a typical Supreme Court jurist: a middle-aged white male who had served as a trial judge for a decade. Sears-Collins, who had originally planned to run a "shoe leather and sweat" campaign to win reelection to the Fulton County Superior Court, joked to a reporter that all she had to do was add 158 more counties.[26]

Sears-Collins had an enormous amount of momentum heading into the campaign. Her appointment had made national news, and the ensuing barrage of media coverage afforded her tremendous name recognition. One poll of Georgia attorneys found that many more were familiar with her than with Boswell, and two-thirds of those surveyed rated her as qualified or well-qualified. Lawyers' opinions are particularly relevant in judicial elections, which are widely ignored by the public at large, though such polls can be influenced by racial and gender bias. In fact, the Atlanta Bar Association's 1992 rankings of the twelve Fulton County superior court judges showed a disparity between lawyers' perceptions of the efficiency and knowledge of the law exhibited by the black judges and objective measures such as their reversal rates and case backlogs.[27]

Both Boswell and Sears-Collins were baffled by Georgians' lack of interest in the race. "Judges are powerful," Boswell stated. "They put people in prison, take houses away, decide which parent will have custody and can shut down a newspaper, all with the stroke of a pen. . . . And yet, people do not seem concerned with who serves as judge." Sears speculated that the low turnout at campaign events reflected the fact that judicial candidates were barred from discussing many issues that stirred people's emotions, such as abortion and the death penalty.[28]

Sears-Collins also had the strong backing of Governor Miller, who launched a vigorous crusade to promote his appointee. Boswell tried to emphasize his experience on the bench and his interest in bringing computer technology to the Supreme Court, but he was "up against more than just Sears-Collins' resources," as a reporter observed. "The fact that she was Miller's choice—and because of her youth, a surprise choice—means that her defeat would be an embarrassment to Miller. . . . Miller says he will do whatever it takes to ensure her victory." Sears-Collins concurred: "He clearly wants to protect his investment." Miller made six campaign appearances for Sears-Collins. She, too, was a swirl of activity—"just about everywhere this political season," according to her erstwhile employer, the *Columbus Ledger-Enquirer*. "Tune into an Atlanta radio station. That's her answering a caller's question. Or ramble up to Lenox Square for a conference on women in politics. She's the keynote speaker. . . . The former Columbus resident hasn't been scarce in Columbus either. She's visited the city four times already during the fledgling political season. And guess who'll be the commencement speaker at Columbus College?"[29]

She was not always received with enthusiasm. At one appearance before a Rotary club, a friend of Miller's introduced her by telling the crowd of white males, "This is the governor's choice. I know y'all may not like it, but things are changing, and if we don't vote for her, there's gonna be somebody else after her. So you're just gonna have to suck it up and take it." Nonetheless, she plowed ahead, giving almost seventy speeches to civic and legal organizations throughout the state in the few months between her appointment and the elections, including campaign appearances in Augusta and Columbus on her June 13 birthday. Her crusade to get the legal profession to increase its use of plain English was garnering national attention, as was her decision in *In re Jane Doe*, which the Georgia Supreme Court (minus Sears-Collins herself) affirmed on July 6.[30]

Campaign funds poured in at a steady clip, allowing Sears-Collins to purchase print and radio advertisements. Fred Tokars, who had served as her finance chair when she ran for the Fulton Superior Court judgeship, and his wife, Sara, made the first major contributions to her campaign, donating twenty-five hundred dollars each. By mid-June, her political contributions had more than tripled the approximately twenty-five thousand dollars Boswell had raised. Although at the start of her campaign Sears-Collins had faced what political pundit Bill Shipp described as the "twin electoral handicaps" of being a black woman, he predicted that the "backing of the Democratic Party power structure, $83,000 in the bank and celebrity status as the nation's only sitting black female state Supreme Court justice have propelled Leah Sears-Collins into strong position to win a July 21 election for a full term on the bench. [Boswell will] have a hard time matching Sears-Collins' ability to make audiences—and the media—swoon. While Boswell talks about placing more court information on floppy disks . . . Sears-Collins is reaching the general public as an exciting populist." She was indeed a captivating, photogenic candidate, and the media responded by chronicling her every move and thought: here was a feature story about her views on linking her children's allowances to chores;

there was a photograph of her riding a tandem bicycle with her husband. Her fondness for skating through Piedmont Park with her family earned her a reputation as "the Rollerblading Justice."[31]

The endorsements started rolling in as well: the *Atlanta Constitution*, the Georgia Association of Educators' Political Action Committee, the *Columbus Ledger-Enquirer*, the *Athens Observer*. They praised the unique perspective her youth, race, and gender brought to the court. They extolled her forthright manner and both her toughness and her compassion. They lauded her academic credentials and her legal experience. And they listed her numerous honors and extracurricular activities, many of which began with the word *founder*: founder of the Columbus Battered Women's Project; founding president of the Georgia Association of Black Women Attorneys; creator of the "You Be the Judge" workshop; chair-elect of the Atlanta Bar Association's Judicial Section and chair of its Minority Clerkship Program; board member of the Sadie G. Mays Nursing Home, the Georgia Chapter of the National Council of Christians and Jews, and the United Way's Drug Abuse Action Committee. She was honored in *Dollars and Sense Magazine*'s "Salute to African-American Business and Professional Women" and featured in Southern Bell's Calendar of Black History. The Southern Christian Leadership Conference gave her its Drum Major for Justice award, while the American Bar Association bestowed on her the Margaret Brent Women Lawyers of Achievement award. She had become a juggernaut.[32]

Boswell, who was well regarded in the legal community, got only scant coverage of his advocacy for information technology and state funding to defend indigent people. He tried to emphasize his experience by distributing a campaign brochure that contrasted his long list of accomplishments with the fact that Sears-Collins had served only on the Atlanta Traffic Court and as a superior court judge. But the brochure only garnered Sears-Collins more attention as the media leaped to describe her reaction to the pamphlet. "I did not get appointed by Gov. Miller by being a traffic court judge. . . . Boswell has been a nice, competent judge and he's been around a long time . . . but I have done a lot in a much shorter period of time." Love Sears-Collins was even more blunt and dismissive, claiming that Boswell had "insulted the judiciary and women by not recognizing her as 'justice' and by misrepresenting his opponent." He described Boswell as launching "a desperate effort to do CPR on a very fledgling campaign effort." Boswell generated some attention a few weeks before the election when he sentenced a hairdresser charged with using cocaine to provide free haircuts at a nursing home, but he just could not compete with Leah Sears-Collins's star power and resources.[33]

The race looked like a squeaker at the end of the day on July 21. The state was using a new, glitchy computer system, and the vote counting progressed at a glacial pace. At first, the rural precincts showed strong support for Boswell, but Sears-Collins pulled ahead when the urban ballots began rolling in. With approximately 60 percent of the votes tabulated by three o'clock the following afternoon, Sears-Collins accepted the Associated Press's declaration that she was the winner. "The secretary of state's office will make you have a heart attack, if you're me—they're so slow and plodding," she said. "I had no idea the counting would take so long and it would come in dribbles like this." When all the votes were tabulated, she had a resounding victory, taking more than 54 percent of the vote, 410,489 to 345,573. She had recorded another first: the first woman in Georgia to win a contested statewide election.[34]

Sears-Collins's victory fit in with what newspapers and magazines were touting as the Political Year of the Woman. A record number of female candidates were running for federal and state offices, and Sears-Collins and many others were convinced that huge gains would occur in November since women were used to participating in politics at the grassroots level. "We are the letter writers, the envelope stuffers. . . . We are the campaign workers, the campaign managers, the campaign organizers," she said. Many of these women candidates, including Carol Moseley Braun, who was running for a U.S. Senate seat from Illinois, chose to seek office after becoming angry at the way the all-male Senate Judiciary Committee had handled the fall 1991 confirmation hearings for U.S. Supreme Court nominee Clarence Thomas. Anita Hill, a former colleague of Thomas's who had gone on to become a law professor at the University of Oklahoma, alleged that he had sexually harassed her at work ten years earlier. Male senators initially brushed off Hill's claims, and the Senate Judiciary Committee was reluctant to launch a formal investigation. Six U.S. congresswomen, including Patsy Mink and Barbara Boxer, and the District of Columbia's nonvoting congressional delegate marched to the Senate to demand that action on Thomas's nomination be delayed until Hill's allegations received a full hearing. In the face of enormous public pressure, the committee finally called Hill to testify on October 11: the televised hearings showed an African American woman facing a hostile panel of fourteen white men who seemed to be judging her rather than the man who was seeking a seat on the nation's highest court. The spectacle of the proceedings led to a national debate about sexual harassment and about the "glass ceiling" that kept women out of office and ultimately inspired women to run for office. Lynn Yeakel, the upset winner of Pennsylvania's Democratic Senate primary, ran campaign commercials that featured footage of her opponent, Republican Arlen Specter, aggressively questioning Hill; Yeakel then asked voters, "Were you as angry about this as I was?" Seattle Municipal Court judge Barbara Madsen concluded that the world would never change until women claimed positions of leadership at all levels and decided to run for a seat on the Washington Supreme Court, provoking laughter from her husband when she announced her intent. When Tacoma attorney Elaine Houghton also decided to seek the post, it marked the first time two women had competed for the same seat on the court. And despite predictions from "progressive" males that the two women would split the "women's vote," Madsen and Houghton finished first and second in the five-way primary, and Madsen ultimately won the seat. Alongside the proliferation of women candidates, reapportionment after the 1990 U.S. Census resulted in the creation of new majority-minority districts that further boosted the chances of black and Hispanic women. When the 103rd Congress was seated in January 1993, the number of women in the House of Representatives had grown from twenty-eight to forty-seven, while the number of women in the Senate tripled as not only Braun but Boxer, Dianne Feinstein, and Patty Murray joined incumbents Barbara Mikulski, who had won reelection, and Nancy Landon Kassebaum. Braun became the nation's first black woman senator. Georgia voters did their part, electing Jackie Barrett as the country's first black female sheriff and sending Cynthia McKinney, the state's first black congresswoman, to Washington.[35]

Sears-Collins and Hill crossed paths in 1992 when the American Bar Association (ABA) Commission on Women in the Profession presented Hill with a special award at the ABA's annual meeting on August 9 in San Francisco. Sears-Collins and four others were honored with the Margaret Brent Women Lawyers of Achievement Award during a luncheon at which the keynote speaker was Hillary Clinton, whose husband was the Democratic Party's nominee for the U.S. presidency.[36]

The presence of Clinton and Hill turned the event into a raucous affair that was more like a sporting event than a lawyers' lunch: tickets were scalped, people stood outside the room holding signs that said "Tickets needed," and more than a thousand people were turned away. Both women got standing ovations and thunderous applause from the twelve hundred lucky ticket-holders, and "the whoops and cheers were of a passion, pitch and timbre never before heard at bar conventions, where women have historically played minor roles and minority women were virtually invisible." The audience was nearly as enthusiastic when Sears-Collins and the other four honorees—Herma Kay Hill, the first woman dean of the law school at the University of California at Berkeley; U.S. Appeals Court judge Betty Fletcher; Nashville lawyer Margaret Behm; and U.S. representative Patsy Mink, who had spearheaded passage of Title IX—received their awards, which were glass pyramids containing shards of glass "to represent women's efforts to shatter the glass ceiling and achieve professional success."[37]

Not everyone was quite as buoyant about the tone of the convention: one man was annoyed that the ABA's "image had been reduced in the media to Hillary Clinton, Anita Hill, and Pro-Choice," and a past ABA president complained that the event favored Democrats over Republicans and Hill's testimony over Thomas's. Helen Nies, chief judge of the Court of Appeals for the Federal Circuit, admitted to an audience at another convention session that she was "not entirely comfortable with Anita Hill as a heroine.... We are not all goody two-shoes . . . a lot of nasty women will use this to advance themselves." Vice President Dan Quayle also criticized the ABA for honoring Hill. Cory Amron, chair of the Commission on Women in the Profession, responded, "I think that the discussion about sexual harassment in the workplace transcends" the debate. She continued, "Just by speaking out [Hill] has had an extraordinary effect on the legal profession." For her part, Leah Sears-Collins watched the Thomas-Hill testimony and saw two articulate, well-dressed, Ivy League–educated African Americans appearing before Congress. She was struck by how much progress her race had made.[38]

The October 1992 issue of *Ebony* declared that it was not only the Year of the

Woman but also the Year of the *Black* Woman. "Sometimes change goes unnoticed in the dizzying pace of daily living," began the cover story. "It is as hushed as a ballot being cast, as quiet as the turn of a page, as silent as the lone tear rolling down the cheek of a triumphant athlete." The feature, which included Sears-Collins, Braun, Barrett, and McKinney in its long list of black women of achievement, celebrated their "power and presence . . . in politics, literature, sports, entertainment, science, education, and religion." Astronaut Mae Jemison had just become the first black woman in outer space. Halle Berry, who in 2002 would become the first black woman to win an Academy Award for Best Actress, had recently broken through as a Hollywood star. Jackie Joyner-Kersee, Gail Devers, and Georgia's Gwen Torrence had earned Olympic gold medals. Books by Toni Morrison, Alice Walker, and Terry McMillan had all spent much of the summer on the *New York Times* Best Seller list. "This is indeed *the* year for many women, and African-American sisters are racking up victories and receiving long overdue recognition in many fields," said Johnetta Cole, the first black woman president of Atlanta's Spelman College.[39]

Less than a week after the November 1992 elections ushered in a record number of women officeholders, the Supreme Court of Georgia doubled its number of women justices when Governor Miller appointed DeKalb Superior Court judge Carol W. Hunstein to fill the seat left vacant by the death of Justice Charles Weltner, a onetime member of the U.S. Congress who had opposed segregation during the turbulent 1960s. The *Atlanta Journal and Constitution* applauded his replacement:

> Judge Hunstein comes to the court with special sensitivities and commitments. As a young, divorced mother, she contracted bone cancer and had to have a leg amputated above the knee. She subsequently attended law school on a scholarship for disabled people.
>
> In her capacity as judge, she co-chaired the DeKalb County task force that helped create the state's most sophisticated program for dealing with domestic violence. More recently, as president of the state judicial council, she chaired the committee that prepared a massive report on gender bias in the judicial system.
>
> That report, which made her some enemies in the more hidebound sections of the legal community, pointed to the need for greater awareness of the nature of domestic violence. And it didn't neglect areas of sexual bias against men, such as in the awarding of child custody in divorce cases.

The Georgia Supreme Court has increasingly become a defender of individual liberties and the rights of the least powerful. This has been especially important at a time when the federal judiciary has swung sharply to the right.[40]

Echoing the assertion that the Georgia Supreme Court had become a guardian of individual rights and liberties, the ABA Journal published "The Changing Faces of Southern Courts" in an issue featuring on its cover Janet Reno, the first woman to serve as U.S. attorney general. The article noted that "nowhere has [change] been more dramatic or swift than in Georgia. . . . The list of decisions by the Georgia Supreme Court that fly in the face of recent conservative federal court rulings is growing by the month." After reading the article, Hillary Clinton, who had recently moved to the White House as First Lady, sent Sears-Collins a note recalling the Women Lawyers of Achievement Awards luncheon and declaring, "I . . . share the excitement I know you must feel to be a part of the Georgia Supreme Court at this time in history." Such cases have a profound impact on the lives of Georgia residents, because when a state's highest court relies on that state's constitution to expand individual rights, the decision cannot be reviewed by the federal courts. This was the "new judicial federalism" advocated by William J. Brennan, the U.S. Supreme Court justice after whom the Sears-Collinses had named their daughter: state jurists relying on their independent state constitutions as a source of law to provide greater rights than those recognized by federal jurists interpreting identical or similarly phrased rights in the U.S. Constitution. For example, the U.S. Supreme Court held in 1991 that a statute requiring dancers to wear pasties and G-strings did not violate the First Amendment since there was a sufficiently important governmental interest in preventing public nudity. The following year, the Georgia Supreme Court declined to follow the U.S. Supreme Court's reasoning and instead relied on the Georgia Constitution's Freedom of Speech Clause in striking down three city ordinances prohibiting liquor sales where nude dancing was performed. In 1993, when the Georgia Supreme Court upheld a more narrowly drawn ordinance prohibiting the sale of alcohol at erotic dance establishments when "limited to adult dance entertainment businesses that studies have shown produce undesirable secondary effects," Sears-Collins dissented, "not because I am a nude dancing enthusiast . . . but because I strongly believe that the rights protected by the First Amendment to the United States Constitution are essential to freedom and democracy, and that those rights have been tread upon in this case without good cause having been shown. . . . I do not believe that unidentified 'studies' constitute sufficient justification for diminishing rights protected by the First Amendment."[41]

But 1992 also brought tragedy to the Sears-Collins family when thirty-nine-year-old Sara Tokars was murdered on November 29 in front of her sons, aged six and four. Sara's husband, Fred, had shared a cubicle with Love Sears-Collins when both men were working for Southern Bell during the 1980s. Fred Tokars, an accountant, was studying for a law degree at night at Woodrow Wilson College of Law, and the couples became friends. Fred Tokars had served as Leah's finance chair when she ran for Fulton Superior Court judge, and Sara helped with the victory party once she was elected to the bench. Shortly thereafter, Leah introduced Fred to Atlanta mayor Andrew Young, and Tokars, who had opened his own criminal and tax law practice in 1986, was appointed a part-time Atlanta municipal judge. Fred Tokars continued to support Leah Sears-Collins and other local political candidates, and he was a major contributor to both Sears-Collins's and Barrett's 1992 campaigns.

Blond, sunny Sara was a gentle soul who seemed to feel more comfortable with children than with Atlanta's political and legal community. Every year, at the Sears-Collins family's Christmas party, Brennan's room would be set up with a movie, games, and cookies so that the kids could have their own little gathering upstairs. Sara often slipped away from the adults to join the children.[42]

When Love and Leah heard about the murder on the morning of November 30, they rushed to the Tokars' house to comfort Fred and the children. Leah embraced Tokars before she left, with cameras recording her gesture of support. But as they drove away, Love said, "Leah, he didn't look at me in the eye. Do you think that there is any way possible he could have had something to do with this?" She dismissed the notion as unthinkable. But within a week, investigators learned that Sara had been afraid of her husband, wanted a divorce, and had hired a private investigator to follow him after finding information in his safe that implicated him and others in illegal activities. She had asked the private investigator to take his files to the police if anything happened to her.[43]

On December 23, Eddie Lawrence, one of Fred Tokars's business associates, and another man, Curtis Rower, were arrested and charged with Sara's kidnapping, robbery, and murder. The following day, Tokars attempted suicide. Rower confessed to being the gunman and said he had been hired by Lawrence, who drove the getaway car. Rower claimed that Lawrence said that Tokars would pay them five thousand dollars to kill Sara. A federal grand jury subpoenaed Tokars's business records in early June, and he was named as an unindicted coconspirator later that month. Sara's family then filed a civil lawsuit to prevent Fred Tokars from receiving Sara's $1.75 million life insurance payout, and on August 25, 1993, he was arrested.

A twenty-two-page indictment accused Tokars and seven other men of running a narcotics and money-laundering enterprise that extended from Detroit to Atlanta and used "kidnapping, torture and murder to protect the continuity of its operations and to protect its members from arrest and prosecution." The charges included racketeering, murder, murder for hire, cocaine trafficking, obstruction of justice, counterfeiting, and money laundering. Tokars was granted a change of venue to the Northern District of Alabama because his defense lawyers believed that the publicity would prevent him from getting a fair trial in Georgia.[44]

The six-week federal trial began on February 28, 1994. The prosecution called Leah Sears-Collins to testify in an attempt to show that Tokars was politically well connected, thus giving Sara a reason to fear that she would be unable to get custody of their sons in a divorce proceeding. When that day arrived, the prosecution asked her one question, as she recalled. "You're Justice Leah Sears?" "Yes." "Thank you." Then it was the defense's turn. "You're on the Supreme Court of Georgia?" "Yes sir, I am." One of the jurors, an African American, soundlessly clapped in approval. After establishing that Sears-Collins had helped Tokars get a seat on the City Court of Atlanta, Bobby Lee Cook asked her if there was anything lower than a traffic court judge. "Yes," she replied, sensing his surprise and consternation at her response. Cook intended to demonstrate that Tokars lacked political clout, and he did not know what was coming. "And what is that?" he asked. "A part-time traffic court judge," she answered. Cook rested. On April 8, 1994, Tokars was convicted of every count against him. He received four sentences of life without parole in a federal prison.[45]

The Tokars episode caused tremendous heartache for Sears-Collins. She was new on the bench, had an "uphill battle to climb with [some of her] colleagues who weren't that welcoming anyway," and the press had trotted her out as one of Tokars's "well-connected" acquaintances. She felt dazed and bruised.[46]

The conclusion of the Tokars trial was not the end of Sears-Collins's personal woes that year. On November 18, 1994, she decided the case of *Williams v. State* as Justice Sears-Collins. By November 21, the opinion in *In re Siemon* identified her as Justice Sears. Leah and Love had decided to get a divorce.[47]

CHAPTER 5

Not Yet a Perfect World

Justice will not come . . . until those who are not injured
are as indignant as those who are injured.
—Thucydides

At the heart of liberty is the right to define one's own concept of existence,
of meaning, of the universe, and of the mystery of human life.
—*Planned Parenthood of Southeastern Pa. v. Casey*

In the center of the house at 38 The Prado in Atlanta's Ansley Park neighborhood is a stained glass window, set in the streetside wall of a large closet that Brennan and Love Sears-Collins once shared. The closet harbors memories. Some are cheerful, like the April Fool's Day when Brennan and Addison placed a bucket of water so that it would soak their father when he opened the closet door. Some are forlorn, like the missing tie rack. Love and Leah's marriage had begun to develop cracks, and the couple separated several times. When they did, the tie rack would disappear. "When are you coming home, Dad?" Brennan would ask. "You'll know I'm home when you see my tie rack hanging again," Love would tell her. So every day during the separations, Brennan would come home from school and run to the closet, hoping that the tie rack would be back. In November 1994, when Brennan was seven, the tie rack left permanently.[1]

Within a month, Love had located his high school sweetheart, Valeda, to whom he had been engaged before he met Leah. Two weeks after Leah and

Love's divorce was granted on September 23, 1995, Love and Valeda married. They remained in Atlanta while Love worked on the 1996 Atlanta Olympics. Shortly thereafter, Love accepted a position at Dillard University in New Orleans. On the day he was to leave, Brennan was sitting in class at Morningside Elementary School when she looked up and saw her father's face in the window. He had come to say good-bye. After pulling her out of class, he held her for a few minutes. "I just want you to know, no matter how far I go from you, I'm never too far away," he said. "I'm going to New Orleans, but I can be on the next flight here if you need me. I can drive here. Whatever you need, I'm here. I'll always be here for you. Please be strong, through everything. I know it's hard, but you have to be strong." Comforted by his words, Brennan recalled them whenever she faced difficult times.[2]

After Love moved out, Onnye Sears moved in. She was needed. Leah's mother took over after-school pickups, hamburger runs, making dinner, and card games with the kids. In addition to her full-time job on the Georgia Supreme Court, Leah was also laboring to finish a master of laws in the judicial process degree at the University of Virginia. Created in 1980, the program was designed for state and federal appellate court judges, and three of Leah's colleagues—Charles Weltner, Robert Benham, and Willis Hunt—had earned the degree. The program consisted of two six-week summer sessions plus a written thesis. Leah had participated in the summers of 1993 and 1994, taking Addison and Brennan with her to Charlottesville and living in a university apartment. The kids had attended Cavalier Day Camp while Leah went to three classes a day on such topics as Law and Economics, Courts and Social Science, and Law and Medicine. Leah loved it: "That's my kind of thing, deconstructing and constructing. It was more than just the cases, it was Why are we here? Where does our jurisprudence come from? How do European systems differ from ours?" Unlike the male participants, most of the eight women in the program brought their children with them. The families were housed close together and bonded over cookouts, and the kids played together in the evenings while their mothers studied. But Love stayed behind in Atlanta.[3]

After the end of the Sears-Collins marriage, Onnye stayed with Brennan and Addison while Leah spent weekends in her office, tackling a topic that aroused her passions. "I knew I'd have to work on something that would draw me in so compellingly that I'd forget about my divorce," she reflected. And so as the calendar turned to 1995, she poured her wounded heart into her thesis, "Female Circumcision: Crime or Culture?" Female circumcision or female genital mutilation (FGM) involves the total or partial excision of the female external genitalia. It is a cultural rite, thousands of years old, performed primarily on girls in Africa, Asia, and the Middle East sometime between infancy and puberty. It ranges from the partial or total removal of the clitoris to infibulation, its most severe form, in which the clitoris, labia minora, and most of the labia majora are excised and the vagina is largely stitched shut. The procedure is generally performed without anesthesia, often under unhygienic circumstances, and can cause serious short- and long-term physical and mental harm. According to 2016 estimates, as many as two hundred million girls have undergone the procedure. When Leah was working on her master's degree, female circumcision was not yet illegal in the United States, where it occurred among some immigrant populations for a variety of cultural, social, and religious reasons, though Congress outlawed it soon thereafter with the 1996 Female Genital Mutilation Act.[4]

Leah's thesis caused her to think about her children and their African roots. "On June 7, 1983, I became forever with child when I gave birth to a beautiful brown baby boy in a steel room in Atlanta, Georgia where one become two," she wrote. "The man to whom I was married at the time, my son's father, gave my baby his name (Addison), gave him his freedom (he cut the umbilical cord), and two days later he took my son from me and saw to it that Addison received the same operation he had had 28 years before.... Even today I wonder whether my son's [circumcision] constitutes child abuse ... or a harmless but important cultural marker identifying my son with his family and our group." She pondered the geographical fortune of eight-year-old Brennan, who was at the age when so many girls were circumcised. "Perhaps the central question in this whole debate is not just the propriety of female circumcision, but why female bodies in virtually every society in the world are subject to alteration, maiming, mutilation, and control." While female circumcision was not an issue for Western women, they faced societal pressures to "diet, dye, and debilitate" by wearing "stilts that pass as shoes" and undergoing cosmetic surgery. The *Atlantic Monthly*, which ran a feature on FGM in 1995, the same year that Leah was writing her dissertation, interviewed her on the subject. "Legal issues concerning FGM are complex," she acknowledged. "Can an adult woman do this to herself? We American women consent to have our breasts enlarged, which is another bizarre thing women do for the pleasure of men. Is that so different? I think we need comprehensive legislation" to prevent FGM.[5]

Though writing the thesis helped Leah purge her soul of grief, one of her life's lowest moments—as well as one of the highest—came on June 13, 1995, her fortieth birthday. Her mother was out of town, her children were with Love, and Leah was at a grocery store buying a frozen entree to heat up for her birthday meal. As she reached into the frozen food case, a young man approached her and said, "I just want to tell you that you are the most beautiful woman I have ever seen!" Leah's mood instantly shifted 180 degrees, and she told him, "You don't know what an angel you are!" And she walked out of the store thinking, "I can do this!"[6]

The much-needed compliment came from someone Leah perceived as gay, and it helped to helped further humanize the members of a group whose cases were appearing before the court with increasing frequency. Leah's attitude about equal rights had been evolving for some time. Her first exposure to the lesbian, gay, bisexual, and transgender (LGBT) community came when she was in college, and her education continued when she served on the municipal court with Judge Larry Paul, a gay man who became one of her many white middle-aged male mentors. In 1993, the Georgia Supreme Court decided a case, *Van Dyck v. Van Dyck*, that involved a man seeking to terminate his alimony obligation because his former wife was sharing a home and consequently expenses with her new lover. The law specified that alimony would be reduced when the recipient remarried or was cohabiting with a person of the opposite sex. In this case, however, the new lover was also a woman. As written, the "plain language" of the law did not apply in the case of a homosexual relationship, and the court ruled that the alimony therefore could not be reduced. Sears wrote a concurrence with the majority's decision in which she acknowledged that alimony is based on an ex-spouse's need and that if that need decreased, the alimony probably should be reduced or terminated: "Logically, it should make no difference whether the ex-spouse has remarried, is living in a meretricious relationship with a person of the opposite sex or is living with a gay partner. In a perfect world it ought to be the financial reality that counts." She continued, "But this is not yet a perfect world. While the relationships of married couples are clearly defined by law, lesbian and gay couples in America today cannot legally marry, no matter how deep their love and how firm their commitment." She went on to explain that since the law did not treat homosexual couples as married when doing so would benefit them (for example, filing taxes jointly or obtaining health insurance as a family), it could not treat them as married to penalize them: "It would not be fair to . . . saddle gay and lesbian couples with a penalty accorded unwed heterosexual couples who live together who have the choice of taking advantage of the benefits of marriage without according homosexual couples who live together the benefits of a relationship that for them can never happen under the law." The woman's attorney saw the concurring opinion as an encouraging sign for the gay community, telling a newspaper reporter, "It's not a breakthrough, but it does acknowledge there are relations between couples of the same sex that are similar to marriage."[7]

In the summer of 1995, Georgia representative Billy McKinney, claiming that gay couples were "repulsive" and "diseased," filed a lawsuit challenging four Atlanta ordinances that were designed to extend rights and benefits to domestic partners and combat discrimination based on sexual orientation. The city was one of thirty-six U.S. municipalities that had taken "baby steps toward the legalization of gay marriage" by "extend[ing] some benefits to, or register[ing] for some official purposes, same-sex domestic partnerships." The Georgia Supreme Court upheld the City of Atlanta's authority to ban discrimination based on sexual orientation in city employment and other city affairs and to create a domestic partnership registry to extend visitation rights in city jails to domestic partners. However, the court struck down the city ordinance that recognized domestic partners as a "family relationship" and made employee benefits "available to a City employee in a comparable manner for a domestic partner . . . as for a spouse." The court found that cities could not enact ordinances defining family relationships since other state statutes defined a dependent "either as a spouse, child, or one who relies on another for financial support," and domestic partners did not meet any of these criteria. According to the court, Atlanta could not expand the definition of *dependent* in a way that violated the Georgia's constitution and other laws.[8]

Sears agreed with the court that the City of Atlanta had the authority to enact the antidiscrimination and registry ordinances but disagreed that the benefits ordinance was invalid. "There is no one general law in this state establishing a uniform definition of 'dependent,'" she wrote, "and the requirements of a domestic partnership certainly indicate that a city employee's domestic partner must rely, at least in part, on the employee for financial support." Assistant city attorney Robin Shahar, one of the lawyers representing the city, vowed to work with the relevant parties on crafting a benefits ordinance that would pass muster with the state's high court. Shahar had a personal interest in such cases: she had been denied employment with the Georgia Department of Law when state attorney general Michael Bowers rescinded a job offer after learning that Shahar was planning a religious commitment ceremony with her same-sex partner. Bowers, who had successfully defended Georgia's prohibition of sodomy before the U.S. Supreme Court, claimed that Shahar's relationship would affect the department's credibility and its ability to enforce the state's antisodomy law. Though Shahar failed to convince a federal appellate court that Bowers lacked the authority to fire an employee under such circumstances, her work with the city council ultimately advanced the interests of Atlanta's gay community. The Atlanta City Council passed an ordinance providing insurance benefits for dependents of city employees registered as domestic partners, defining a *dependent* as "one who relies on another for financial support." The new ordinance withstood a legal challenge, with the Georgia Supreme Court upholding it and noting that the city had carefully followed the court's ruling by eliminating from the ordinance's definition of *dependent* any language recognizing any new family relationship similar to marriage.[9]

In 1996, Sears made her mark on yet another "gay case" when the Georgia Supreme Court was called on to decide whether the Georgia laws that criminalized sodomy and the solicitation of sodomy violated the state's constitution. L. Chris Christensen, whom a jury had convicted of soliciting a male undercover officer for oral sex, claimed that the law violated the rights to privacy and free speech protected by the state constitution. Christensen challenged the conviction under the state constitution because the U.S. Supreme Court's 1986 *Bowers v. Hardwick* decision had declared that Georgia's antisodomy statute did not violate the U.S. Constitution. In a brief opinion, the Georgia Supreme Court reached the same conclusion as the *Bowers* court, finding that "the proscription against sodomy is a legitimate and valid exercise of state police power in furtherance of the moral welfare of the public," that the law prohibiting the solicitation of unlawful acts did not violate free speech rights, and that even though more than half of the states had decriminalized consensual sodomy (including seven by judicial decree), "the right to determine what is harmful to health and morals or what is criminal to the public welfare belongs to the people through their elected representatives." Sears and Justice Carol W. Hunstein wrote dissenting opinions, with both women arguing that the majority had incorrectly applied the "rational basis" test in evaluating Christensen's right to privacy claim when it should have applied the "compelling state interest" test. When the rational basis test is applied, the party challenging the law must show that there is no rational basis for the statute. It is a difficult hurdle to overcome, and courts using the rational basis test almost always uphold the constitutionality of the laws in question. Conversely, the compelling state interest test begins with a presumption that the law is unconstitutional and requires the government to show that the legislature had a compelling interest sufficient to overcome a constitutional right. A court applies the compelling state interest test when an enacted law substantially infringes on a fundamental right. Both justices believed that the state had not met its burden of proof under this test.[10]

Sears, however, went much further, writing an impassioned dissent that was more than five times as long as the majority's opinion: "Throughout history, the impulse of a majority to impose its moral judgments upon the rest of society often has resulted in laws that violate the fundamental tenets of our constitutional democracy. Among these tenets are the inalienable right to be left alone so long as one's private conduct does not interfere with the rights of others." She asserted that the only argument the state had made to support its position was its moral interest in condemning acts of homosexual sodomy, but "case law clearly shows that the constitutionality of a criminal statute is not established merely by alleging that it comports with the morals of a majority. For example, [in 1967] laws prohibiting interracial marriage were declared unconstitutional even though a majority believed that miscegenation was a moral offense with ancient roots." Moreover, she added, the record did not show that most Georgians believed consensual, noncommercial, private acts of sodomy between consenting adults to be immoral. In fact, the Georgia Supreme Court had gotten fifteen amici curiae ("friend of the court") briefs from religious organizations and leaders in support of Christensen. "Sexual conduct in private between consenting adults is a matter of private morality to be instructed by religious precept or ethical example and persuasion, rather than by legal coercion," she concluded. "I believe that the result of the majority opinion is pathetic and disgraceful, and has tragic implications for the constitutional rights of the citizens of this State."[11]

Sears was becoming well-known for her colorful, passionate, and occasionally funny written opinions. "I believe opinions should set a tone. I think opinions can be and should be sad, angry, or remorseful. I want people to see who I am and how I think through my opinions," she said in 1993, though she acknowledged that "every time I bang out an opinion that may outrage someone, I wonder if this is the opinion that creates the noose that could kill my chances for advancement to a higher court." Sears thus made no secret of the fact that she was interested in moving up the judicial ladder, and observers frequently speculated that the White House would tap her for a federal appellate court position.[12]

Seven months after her *Christensen* dissent, the Stonewall Bar Association of Georgia asked her to deliver the keynote address at the group's annual awards dinner. The association, composed of legal professionals who support the rights of LGBT people, was named for the Stonewall Inn, a New York City gay bar that was the site of 1969 riots that marked the beginning of the U.S. gay rights movement. Sears spoke to the association about flame bearers: "leaders whose heat and light both warm and illuminate the paths of those who seek to advance unpopular causes." And although she sought not to advance a cause but to interpret the law as she saw it, the LGBT community had come to see her as a flame bearer. "I do not like discrimination against anybody based on characteristics that they were born with and can't do anything about," she later told a journalist. "It's so fundamentally un-American, I feel it in every cell of my body. And that is the theme of my life."[13]

In November 1998, just two years after the *Christensen* decision, the Georgia Supreme Court reversed itself. Noting that the right of privacy guaranteed by the Georgia Constitution is "far more extensive that the right of privacy protected by the U.S. Constitution," the court held in *Powell v. State* that the state's antisodomy statute was unconstitutional "insofar as it criminalizes the performance of private, unforced, non-commercial acts of sexual intimacy between persons legally able to consent." Though *Powell* involved consensual heterosexual sodomy, the decision decriminalized homosexual sexual activity as well. Sears, elated that a majority of the Georgia Supreme Court had "fulfilled its constitutional responsibility," termed Justice Robert Benham's majority opinion "inspired." Perhaps drawing on her own experience, she added, "There will, of course, be those who will criticize today's decision, and who may even seek to demonize some members of this Court for their legal analysis. This pattern of personally attacking and pillorying individuals who disagree with certain positions, rather than engaging in constructive ideological discourse with them, has regrettably become more and more prevalent in our culture. Those who would make such personal attacks, however, do not fully appreciate that all of my colleagues, those who agree with the majority as well as those who dissent, are honorable and decent jurists who struggle to fulfill their constitutional responsibilities to the people of this State."[14] By that time, Sears had her own extensive experience with personal attacks.

———

Haskell George Ward was irritated. The associate magistrate had asked Justice Benham to speak at a Griffin Rotary Club meeting on August 28, 1997. They had a tenuous connection: Benham had roomed with Ward's former college roommate, Freeman Walker, while attending law school at the University of Georgia. Benham had accepted the invitation but canceled at the last minute and asked Leah Sears to replace him. Ward had never heard of Sears, and he was none too happy with the substitution. Sears herself was less than enthusiastic, despite the fact that she had included in her tongue-in-cheek "Best of a Supreme" list that "you get to speak to every Rotary and Kiwanis Club in the state."[15]

When Sears drove to the county courthouse and met Ward, both were pleasantly surprised. She was not expecting to see a handsome black man, and he was not expecting to see a beautiful, stylish woman driving a white convertible. She was further intrigued when she entered his chambers and saw two photos of a grinning young man standing next to a rhinoceros, asking, "Is that you? Is that a real rhinoceros?" Ward told her the story behind the pictures. Though Ward had now returned his hometown, Griffin, he had traveled extensively.[16]

Ward was born on March 13, 1940, in a three-room house in the segregated town of Griffin, where part of *Driving Miss Daisy* was filmed. His parents divorced the year after he was born, and he was raised by his hardworking but poor maternal grandmother, Lonnie White. Concerned that Ward would get into trouble while she was working as a maid, White instructed Ward to sit on the porch until she returned home. Teacher Corene Prothro lived two doors away, and she made sure that he followed his grandmother's edict.[17]

Unmotivated to learn, Ward failed the first and second grades. Prothro nevertheless remained convinced that Ward had ability and finally vowed to "split his head open and put the book in it" if he didn't start working. "I thought she would actually do that," he recalled. "In fact, her personality was such that she was capable of breaking your head open and putting the book in it." So Ward straightened up, began earning As and Bs, and was voted "Best All-Around Student and Most Likely to Succeed" by the time he graduated from Fairmont High School in 1959.[18]

Ward went on to attend Clark College in Atlanta (now Clark Atlanta University), where his professors quickly recognized him as a serious student. He participated in the sit-ins of the 1960s, became a student leader, and accepted a job as a student assistant to C. Eric Lincoln, author of *The Black Muslims in America*, who introduced Ward to civil rights activist Malcolm X. When the university got the opportunity to send a student to Kenya, Ward was selected. Ward was studying to become a psychologist and did not want to go, but Lincoln insisted, and in 1962 Ward found himself in Washington, D.C., at an orientation program for Operation Crossroads Africa, where he met President John F. Kennedy. "You're going to meet my friend Tom Mboya," Kennedy told Ward. "And when you meet my friend Tom Mboya, you tell him that we're going to bring some more students over." Mboya had toured North America in 1959, seeking scholarships for East African students, and had met the up-and-coming U.S. senator from Massachusetts during his visit. Kennedy helped arrange to have the Joseph P. Kennedy Jr. Foundation pledge financial support for 250 students in 1960. Ward indeed met Mboya, who became an influential government official after Kenya achieved independence in 1963, and the two men were together on July 4, 1969, the day before Mboya was assassinated.[19]

Ward spent the summer of 1962 building classrooms in Kenya and checking out rhinoceroses and other wildlife in Uganda. His interests shifted from individual to social dynamics, and the trajectory of his life changed. He cried when the time came to go home at the end of the summer, and when he was back in the States, he wrote to Sargent Shriver, the director of the Peace Corps, which had been founded in 1961, to request a position in East Africa. Shriver did not yet have a program in East Africa but offered to send Ward to Ethiopia. So in 1963, after three months of training at the University of California at Los Angeles, Ward joined the second team of Peace Corps volunteers in Ethiopia.[20]

Sears was astonished to hear about Ward's stint in the Peace Corps. Her maternal uncle, Elliott Roundtree, had been a member of the first Peace Corps team sent to Ethiopia in 1962. Since Peace Corps volunteers serve abroad for two years, the two men had overlapped and knew one another. After his stint in Peace Corps, Ward had earned a master's degree in African studies from UCLA in 1967 and had gone on to work for the Ford Foundation in New York City and Nigeria, where he specialized in economic development programs and strategies for the Middle East and Africa. He joined Jimmy Carter's presidential administration, serving as deputy assistant to secretary of state Cyrus Vance from 1977 to 1979, before becoming a deputy mayor of New York City under Ed Koch. In 1989, Ward published *African Development Reconsidered: New Perspectives from the Continent*, a book analyzing Africans' perceptions of their political and socioeconomic problems and the initiatives designed to overcome those problems. In 1991, he helped write and produce a documentary series, *In Search of the American Dream: A Story of the African-American Experience*, hosted by Arthur Ashe, the first African American man to win the U.S. Open and Wimbledon tennis championships. Ashe and Ward had lived a few houses apart in 1965–66 when Ashe was attending UCLA on a tennis scholarship and Ward was pursuing his graduate degree. The six-part series, which aired on the A&E cable network, began with a focus on Ward's childhood in Griffin in the 1940s and 1950s. When Ward traveled to Griffin to film the first segment, he saw that the town was beginning to offer new opportunities for African Americans, and he decided to move back home. Six years later, Chief Magistrate Rita Cavanaugh tapped Ward to become Spalding County's first black judge. He began his four-year term in January 1997.[21]

Instantly smitten, Ward introduced Sears to the Griffin Rotary Club as a woman who might well be a contender for the U.S. Supreme Court. His statement was not groundless flattery; just a few months earlier, Sears had joined three others on President Bill Clinton's short list for a seat on the Eleventh U.S. Circuit Court of Appeals. Sears's speech centered on her concerns about society's cultural decline, particularly the decay of the family. She sounded the alarm about the increase in illegitimate births and bemoaned the fate of children raised in single-parent families, a topic that became a theme of her later speeches. And then she drove home in her white convertible to her own single-parent family.[22]

Ward wasted no time in phoning Sears to thank her for speaking—and to ask her to drive down the next weekend to visit him. She initially agreed but called him back a few minutes later after having second thoughts. So Ward drove to Atlanta to see Sears. During their first date at the Buckhead Diner, he informed Sears that he would like to "pursue a serious relationship" with her and that he believed she was going to be his wife. It was "almost like a board meeting," he recalled. But she was game. He had an impressive résumé, and she was intrigued by his courage. "Most men would have been too scared of me to be so bold, particularly on the first date," she recalled. Still, she proceeded cautiously, she said, "to ensure a ladylike distance from the first date to the next." Ward persuaded Sears to watch his documentary, which she thought "a beautiful series," and he introduced her to a world with which she was barely acquainted: the history, culture, politics, and economics of the African continent. Sears was impressed enough with Ward's intelligence and political acumen to ask him to serve as her campaign manager. He returned that vote of confidence by working round-the-clock to send faxes and letters on her behalf, and his efforts won her over: "He never stopped. That was it for me. That was true love."[23]

The 1998 campaign was her most vicious race to date. Once again, Sears found herself running against an opponent, although the settlement in the Brooks litigation over Georgia's method of choosing judges was supposed to have eliminated such elections for trial and appellate court judges. The goal of the proposed settlement was more diversity in Georgia's courts, but the method of achieving that goal had quickly came under fire. The Missouri Plan would have shifted power from the voters to the governor, and some legal commentators noted that this system had created the state's racial problems. Although judicial selection in Georgia was ostensibly by nonpartisan election, judges customarily resigned before their terms ended, allowing the governor to appoint interim judges. Interim judges were subject to challenge in open elections at the expiration of their terms of office, but since more than half of Georgia's incumbent judges never faced opposition in elections that attracted few voters, appointees were highly likely to stay in office. The result was a de facto appointment system, critics claimed. In response, the governor's office pointed out that the need to garner a majority of the vote in mostly white counties deterred the small pool of qualified black lawyers from seeking judgeships and made governors hesitant to appoint them. Although few judges faced opposition, black candidates running statewide or in rural areas frequently faced off against white candidates.[24]

The black legal community was split. The Georgia Association of Black Women Attorneys supported the Brooks settlement, but the Georgia Alliance of African-American Attorneys, representing 85 percent of Georgia's black lawyers, did not. The Alliance filed an objection to the plan, citing among its concerns the possibility that future governors would not be committed to racial diversity on the bench and that retention elections would still enable white majorities to vote black appointees out of office. The U.S. Justice Department approved the proposal, but it had to be approved by the district court before it could be put into effect.[25]

Federal judge B. Avant Edenfield of the Southern District of Georgia refused to approve the settlement, noting that cases may not be settled when the terms of the proposal violate the law. Georgia voters had an express statutory and constitutional right to elect judges of their choice through contested nonpartisan open elections. Although a three-judge district court had previously found that the current system of electing judges might dilute the strength of black voters in violation of the Voting Rights Act, the defendants had not admitted liability, and no court had determined that Georgia's judicial election laws violated federal law. Nor could Edenfield say with certainty that the plaintiffs were likely to win on that issue. Since the proposed transfer of power from the electorate to the governor and the Judicial Nominating Committee (whose members were appointed by the governor) would fundamentally change Georgia's judicial electoral system, the settlement would violate Georgia's constitution and laws.[26]

Edenfield also held that the mandate of at least thirty African American superior and state court judges by the end of the year violated the Equal Protection Clause of the Fourteenth Amendment to the U.S. Constitution. While not all racial classifications are unconstitutional, they must be justified by a compelling government interest. In addition, the means must be narrowly tailored to achieve the state's goal. Edenfield found ample evidence that Georgia had discriminated against blacks in the legal and judicial fields and felt that a narrowly tailored plan designed to remedy the effects of the state's discriminatory history was warranted. However, the strict quota dictated by the plan was too blunt an instrument and did not pass constitutional muster, he decreed.[27]

With the Missouri Plan off the table, the 1998 judicial elections proceeded under the old system. On May 1, the deadline for qualifying to run in the July 21 nonpartisan primary, two attorneys, William Aynes and George Weaver, came forward to challenge Sears. Aynes quickly faded into the woodwork, but Weaver waged an aggressive campaign. He distributed an election campaign flier attacking Sears's opinions in *Van Dyck v. Van Dyck* and *Christensen v. State*, claiming that she would "require the State to license same-sex marriages" and that she had "referred to traditional moral standards as 'pathetic and disgraceful.'" He also intimated that she opposed the death penalty by saying that "Justice Sears has called the electric chair 'silly.'" In a *National Law Journal* article, Sears had indeed said that electrocution was a silly method of execution, but she had continued, "Why the electric chair, and why not lethal injection or a bullet to the head?" She had also stated that she thought that the people being executed probably deserved it, though she found death penalty cases the most gut-wrenching to decide.[28]

On June 1, the Judicial Qualifications Commission (JQC) received two complaints that Weaver's brochure violated Canon 7 of the Code of Judicial Conduct, which stated in part that candidates for judicial office "shall not use or participate in the use of any form of public communication which the candidate knows or reasonably should know is false, fraudulent, misleading, deceptive, or which contains a material misrepresentation of fact or law or omits a fact necessary to make the communication considered as a whole not materially misleading or which is likely to create an unjustified expectation about results the candidate can achieve."

Georgia's judicial canons had been modified after the 1996 elections, when a candidate for a seat on the Court of Appeals ran a television attack ad excoriating the incumbent for voting to reverse "on a technicality" the conviction of a child molester. The JQC promulgated new standards to prevent candidates from mischaracterizing court opinions for political gain and formed a special committee to deal with complaints of violations.[29]

The special committee determined that the complaints against Weaver had merit, and on June 11 it issued a confidential cease-and-desist request to the candidate. Weaver agreed to comply with the request and revised the brochure's language, but then he ran a television ad that stated, "A conservative who believes in traditional families and morality, George Weaver is standing up for us. What does Justice Leah Sears stand for? Same-sex marriage. . . . And she called the electric chair silly." Though she was repeatedly asked to comment, Sears declined, citing the portion of Canon 7 that prohibited judges from making "statements that would commit or appear to commit them to issues likely to come before the court." A gay political consultant working with Sears's campaign pointed out that Weaver's brochure suggested that he had already taken a position on same-sex marriage and the death penalty, which were controversies likely to come before the court. Sears then ran an ad claiming that *Atlanta Journal* columnist Jeff Dickerson had criticized Weaver's television ad as "shameful, unethical and outright lying." In fact, what the columnist had actually said was that Weaver's first brochure was "shameful, possibly unethical," and "ugly politicking bordering on outright lying." Sears later apologized for her ad after the JQC received a complaint.[30]

Weaver's attacks were of a variety that had been receiving national attention and had spawned a debate about the problems associated with selecting judges through the election process. A *Washington Post* column by David Broder cited Sears's campaign and judicial races in three other states as troubling examples of political retaliation for court opinions that offended the public. "For judges—who are sworn to uphold the Constitution even against public opinion—these are ominous warnings. For the rest of us, they are a signal to remember that freedom and judicial independence are inseparable," he admonished. The *New York Times* also reported on the Sears-Weaver dustup and noted that judicial campaigns in several of the states that elected judges had become "mudslinging matches," inducing judicial disciplinary panels to "do something unique in American politics: forc[e] candidates to stop calling each other lazy, corrupt or soft on crime, unless they can prove it." However, the article continued, the truthfulness-and-integrity drive had spawned critics who "say it not only limits candidates' First Amendment right to political expression but also . . . threatens to curtail the information that voters need to make informed choices."[31]

Sears's predecessor on the Supreme Court, George T. Smith, disagreed that Weaver's campaign was furnishing Georgia's voters with relevant information: "The bench is not a place for catch phrases and slogans or out-of-context quotes," wrote Smith, who joined two law school deans and an attorney in writing a letter published by the *Fulton County Daily Report*, Georgia's daily legal newspaper. "As political conservatives, we also believe that the best way to maintain the integrity [of the courts] is to elect judges who will follow the law, not advance a personal or political agenda." The letter went on to accuse Weaver of grossly mischaracterizing Sears's opinions, which were "well-reasoned and defensible" and "hardly an example of judicial extremism." The authors wanted to go on record as supporting Sears since ethics guidelines prevented her from defending herself. "As conservatives, we appreciate Justice Sears' fidelity to the law, despite our occasional disagreements with the current state of that law, her strong commitment toward the equality of all people in the eyes of the law, her legal scholarship and her devotion to the people of Georgia."[32]

A JQC committee investigated the complaints about Weaver's television ad and determined that it violated the cease-and-desist request regarding Weaver's original brochure. On July 15, therefore, it issued a statement asking the media to publicize the committee's finding that Weaver had intentionally and blatantly violated the request and deliberately engaged in "unethical, unfair, false and intentionally deceptive" campaign practices." Rule 27 authorized the committee immediately to release this type of public statement if its cease-and-desist request was ignored. The following day, Weaver sued the members of the committee and the director of the JQC in federal court, claiming that they had violated his right to free speech by enforcing unconstitutional provisions of the Code of Judicial Conduct. That same year, a similar lawsuit from Minnesota pitting the right of free speech against the state's interest in maintaining an independent and impartial judiciary began winding its way to the U.S. Supreme Court.[33]

Sears trounced both Weaver and Aynes on July 21, taking 54 percent of the vote to retain her seat on the court. Weaver received just under 28 percent, while Aynes, who had done virtually no campaigning, received a little over 18 percent. Weaver claimed that his campaign had been damaged by the JQC's public censure and contended that a runoff would have been necessary if the commission had not rebuked his advertisement, and he asked the court to set aside the election and order a new one.[34]

The district court denied the request on the grounds that there was no evidence of voter fraud or any other circumstance that would have warranted a special election. However, the court agreed that the challenged portion of Canon 7 impermissibly restricted Weaver's right to free speech. Despite the state's compelling interest in maintaining the integrity and independence of its judiciary, Canon 7 restricted too much speech. Its language was so broad that it would apply even to misleading statements negligently made. Consequently, many candidates would feel pressure to stay silent on matters of any consequence for fear of making a factual misstatement that could result in disciplinary action.[35]

While the case was on appeal to the U.S. Court of Appeals for the Eleventh Circuit, the U.S. Supreme Court struck down the "announce clause" in Minnesota's canon of judicial conduct, which prohibited a judicial candidate from "announcing his or her views on disputed legal or political issues." The Court of Appeals agreed with the district court that Canon 7 restricted too much speech, noting that "the Supreme Court's decision [in the Minnesota case] suggests that the standard for judicial elections should be the same as the standard for legislative and executive elections." Judicial candidates across the nation would no longer be above the political fray.[36]

Sears brushed the political dirt from her judicial robes and settled back into her work with a court that was attracting attention from legal scholars following the *Powell* decision for its shift "if not to the left, at least more toward the center." The seven justices, who had been serving together for four years, were viewed as comfortably familiar with each other. And although they sometimes disagreed vehemently with each others' interpretations of the law, they appreciated the rigorous intellectual effort that went into crafting logical opinions on the important issues that came before the court. As Sears quipped, "An opinion is like the dissent, minus a few harsh words." Sears and other jurists might disagree on a particular point but might be allies on a different issue. The seven justices had become accustomed to forming disparate coalitions, and they recognized each other as hardworking jurists of good faith. Sears's concurrence in the *Powell* decision sought not only to explain her belief that the court

had protected the state constitution's guarantee of the right to privacy but also
to advocate for civility and constructive discussion rather than an onslaught
of personal attacks to which she anticipated she and her colleagues would be
subjected. Though they often found themselves debating opposing viewpoints,
Justice George Carley, the lone justice who "respectfully, but vigorously" dissented in *Powell*, was one of Sears's most treasured friends on the court. "I know
that she is reaching her opinion based on her interpretation of the law," Carley
affirmed. "We're the court of last resort. Every case has been to at least one
court, sometimes the court of appeals, too. It comes down to a policy decision.
It's not a political decision ever. This is why she and I are close. She never starts
out saying I want to reverse this case. Sometimes the result we end up with
because that is what the law commands is not the result we would like."[37]

But Sears was also not afraid to voice her sentiments when she felt the situation warranted it, as she did when she was writing the court's opinion in
a case involving Fleet Finance, the state's largest lender of second mortgages.
Three plaintiffs had sued, alleging that Fleet had charged them usurious rates
for home equity loans, in violation of state law, which made it a misdemeanor
to charge a rate of interest that exceeded 5 percent per month. The debtors
claimed that the phrase "per month" meant that interest must be calculated for
each individual month of the loan. Fleet claimed that the figure should be calculated based on the ratio of total interest paid to the total number of months
in the loan.

Taking origination fees, points, and other front-end costs into consider-
ation, the three lead plaintiffs paid interest rates ranging between 22 and 27
percent, according to their interpretation. Fleet's reading of the law, which
required averaging all the finance charges over the life of the loan, reduced the
interest rate to under 2 percent.

Writing for the majority, Sears noted that even though the statute was being
considered in a civil context, the law had to be construed strictly against criminal liability. Moreover, if the statute was subject to more than one reasonable
interpretation, the court must find in favor of the party facing criminal liability.
Under the constraints of the rules of statutory construction, the court held that
the loans were legal and reversed the lower court's denial of Fleet's motion to dismiss the case. No one on the court liked the outcome, but the majority acknowledged it was not the court's place to rewrite the statute. However, ever-mindful

of the impact of her decisions on those who appeared before her, Sears penned dicta that "all but lobbied the state legislature to change the lending laws" that permitted what many observers viewed as predatory loans. "We do not condone Fleet's interest-charging practices, which are widely viewed as exorbitant, unethical, and perhaps even immoral, and suggest that further regulation of the lending industry is needed by our General Assembly to insure the economic survival of individuals like the appellees," she wrote. Sears's fellow justices concurred with her withering critique of Fleet's lending practices, though dissenting justice Robert Bennett would have reached a different result, arguing that the opinion would bring "financial ruin to thousands of households" by allowing lenders to charge interest rates of up to 60 percent per year.[38]

Sears's profound sensitivity to the practical implications of the court's decisions earned her an invitation to preside over landlord-tenant court after she persuaded her colleagues to exclude some lower courts from a new Supreme Court rule requiring that corporations be represented by attorneys in all legal actions. The case that gave rise to the rule was a trade-name dispute, and the plaintiff, a sole proprietorship, had been represented by one of its corporate officers. After finding in favor of the plaintiff, the Supreme Court joined most other jurisdictions in holding that while a natural person has a constitutional right to self-representation, corporations do not. In the future, only licensed attorneys would be authorized to represent corporations in proceedings in a court of record (that is, one that records its proceedings). Mom-and-pop corporations, however, would get a pass as long as the legal action occurred in more informal courts that did not record their proceedings—magistrate courts, administrative tribunals, and most city and municipal courts.[39]

"I commend the majority's foresight in recognizing that a per se prohibition against pro se appearances by corporations is not necessary in certain tribunals, and might, in fact, impose undue hardships," wrote Sears in a concurring opinion. Magistrate Louis Levenson subsequently invited Sears to spend a few hours presiding over his court, wanting her to see "how important [her empathetic] action was in his court, where lawyers, even for the landlords, are a rare sight." While Sears immediately accepted the challenge, the experience was not novel for her: she routinely sat in on lower court cases about four times per year. Sears believed that the practice gave her a feel for dealing with people, let her see how cases were routinely handled across the state, and educated her about the different customs followed in each courthouse: "These are small differences, sometimes curious, but good to know. These are things I'll share with my colleagues when I get back. . . . [Y]ou've got to get out of the ivory tower from time to time for your training and education."[40]

════════════

On April 18, 1999, all the members of the Supreme Court got out of the ivory tower to witness the merger of Atlanta's newest power couple, Leah Sears and Haskell Ward. Leah's views on the importance of stable families had caused her to remain cautious about making her relationship with Haskell permanent and to do extensive research on blended families, but, after a year and a half of dating and Ward's repeated proposals, Sears agreed that it was time. They chose to hold the ceremony at Villa Christina, a popular wedding venue with terraces, gardens, and a stacked stone pavilion. Rather than walking up the aisle through the crowd as most couples do, Sears and Ward approached their guests from the front, descending dramatically from the rolling hill behind the pavilion to the strains of a harp. Fifteen-year-old Addison and twelve-year-old Brennan, who carried the bouquet, preceded them.

They also broke with tradition by taking each other's last names as their middle names: she became Leah Ward Sears, and he became Haskell Sears Ward. And in the eyes of her children, the "alien who appeared one day, hypnotized their mother and set up camp in their home, toting his organic food, reggae music, incense and all things African" became a devoted stepfather who broadened their world immensely.[41]

CHAPTER 6

A Splendid Torch

Our judges should never be beholden to any constituency.
—U.S. Supreme Court justice Sandra Day O'Connor

Leah Ward Sears had to make a choice. It was 2004 and she was about to run in the first major election during which Georgia's judicial candidates would be free to make known their views on controversial legal and political issues, just like any other political candidate. Concerned that the state's judicial elections would become overly politicized in the aftermath of the 2002 federal cases *Republican Party v. White* and *Weaver v. Bonner*, a nonpartisan coalition of lawyers and other professionals had formed the Georgia Committee for Ethical Judicial Campaigns. The committee was asking the 2004 statewide judicial candidates to sign a pledge to conduct their campaigns in a way that would maintain public trust in the integrity, autonomy, and impartiality of the judicial system. The document included pledges to refrain from announcing positions on matters that could come before the court and to avoid making false or misleading statements. Sears, who as presiding justice was slated to become chief justice in 2005, was facing her toughest competition yet in Grant Brantley, a former Cobb County trial judge whose judicial career began in 1980 when he trounced an incumbent. Brantley had strong connections to the Republican Party and was backed by Governor Sonny Perdue, also a Republican. Perdue was incensed that Sears had in 2003 joined a majority opinion holding that the attorney general, not the governor, controlled the state's legal affairs. Soon after taking office in January 2003, Perdue had ordered Georgia attorney general Thurbert Baker to dismiss the state's appeal to the U.S. Supreme Court in a case involving legislative reapportionment under the Voting Rights Act. When Baker refused, Perdue asked the court to declare that the governor's office had the power to order Baker to drop the case. Instead, Sears and four of her colleagues held that under the Georgia Constitution, the attorney general's office had the authority to determine such legal matters. Displeased with the result, Perdue made it no secret that he wanted to see Sears defeated. Addressing a January 2004 Christian Coalition event, Perdue urged the audience to back judges who would "represent mainstream Georgia, mainstream Georgia values, and who will not try to legislate from the bench." Republican leaders had been actively recruiting someone to challenge Sears, the only justice up for reelection in 2004. The party had gained control of the governor's office and the state senate, and the judiciary was the final frontier. Although judicial elections were officially nonpartisan, Brantley's Republican bona fides were unquestionable. He had campaigned as a Republican when he ran for the superior court in 1980, before judicial races became nonpartisan. His campaign manager, Paul Bennecke, had taken a leave of absence from his job as political director of the Georgia Republican Party to work on Brantley's campaign, and his finance director, Patti Peach, was a former Perdue fund-raiser.[1]

Sears signed the Committee for Ethical Judicial Campaigns pledge. Brantley did not, declaring, "I'm not going to sign away my First Amendment rights to some self-appointed committee. It sounds like a protect-the-incumbents committee." That stance freed him to fill out a Christian Coalition survey sent to all the candidates for Georgia's appellate courts. The survey provided short excerpts from the majority and dissenting opinions of five U.S. Supreme Court cases dealing with such subjects as abortion, homosexual conduct, and public school prayer. The candidates were then asked to indicate which opinion they agreed with most. The Christian Coalition, a tax-exempt group prohibited from endorsing political candidates, planned to distribute the results to 750,000 Georgians in a voter guide, describing the survey as a nonpartisan attempt to provide information about the candidates' judicial philosophies. In contrast, Bill Ide, chair of the Georgia Committee for Ethical Judicial Campaigns, believed that the questionnaire was designed to reveal how a candidate would rule on a particular issue in a future case. According to Ide, "The intent is clear that they want judges in their corner on their issue. Legislators can be lobbied, but we're very concerned that judges be fair and impartial and base decisions on the merits of a case when they walk into court." Sears responded to the survey with a letter explaining that her personal views on the issues were irrelevant to her job as a judge, which was to uphold the law. This "could open up the floodgates for the judicial campaigns of the future," she wrote. "Special interest groups would begin to weigh in, and many of those groups won't care about a judge's credentials, qualifications, character or integrity. They will care about just one thing: If they bring a case, will the judge vote their way, or not?" Sears also enclosed an analysis of her judicial philosophy prepared by University of North Carolina political science professor Brian Harrell Harbour, a lawyer and specialist on state supreme courts who had studied all of her opinions and rejected the claim that she was a "judicial extremist."[2]

Among the nine judicial candidates, only Brantley and Mike Sheffield responded to the questionnaire. Sheffield was one of seven candidates vying for an open seat on the Georgia Court of Appeals. Both indicated that they agreed with the dissent to *Lawrence v. Texas*, the 2003 U.S. Supreme Court decision that invalidated state sodomy laws. The Georgia Christian Coalition then distributed the results of its survey, noting that Sears had voted with the majority in *Powell v. State*, the 1998 Georgia Supreme Court decision that overturned the state's law criminalizing sodomy.[3]

"One would have assumed it would be much more appropriate to ask candidates about whether they plan to uphold the U.S. and Georgia Constitutions [and] make determinations based on the law rather than their personal beliefs," grumbled the *Rome News-Tribune*, which then quoted Sears's concurring opinion in *Powell* to bolster its point:

> Simply because something is beyond the pale of "majoritarian morality" does not place it beyond the scope of constitutional protection. To allow the moral indignation of a majority (or, even worse, a loud and/or radical minority) to justify criminalizing private consensual conduct would be a strike against freedoms paid for and preserved by our forefathers. Majority opinion should never dictate a free society's willingness to battle for the protection of its citizens' liberties. To allow such a thing would, in and of itself, be an immoral and insulting affront to our constitutional democracy.[4]

Marc Yeager, president of the Georgia Log Cabin Republicans, doubted that his party would "play by the rules." The organization, which is involved with the concerns of the gay and lesbian community, agreed with its Democratic equivalent, the Georgia Stonewall Democrats, that Sears's opinions on gay issues would likely be used as a "divisive wedge" in state politics. This was hardly idle conjecture since Republican legislators had been quoting Sears's opinions as a reason for needing a state constitutional amendment banning gay marriage.[5]

The debate over same-sex marriage had reached a national crescendo after the U.S. Supreme Court's 2003 *Lawrence v. Texas* decision invalidated sodomy laws nationwide. And although the Court's opinion pointed out that the case did not involve the issue of "whether the government must give formal recognition to any relationship that homosexual persons seek to enter," less than five months later, the Supreme Court of Massachusetts quoted *Lawrence* when it held that same-sex couples had a state constitutional right to civil marriage: "Our obligation is to define the liberty of all, not to mandate our own moral code." The Massachusetts legislature then attempted to create a civil union status that would be equal to marriage, but the state's Supreme Court held that this violated the "equal protection and due process requirements of the Constitution of the Commonwealth and the Massachusetts Declaration of Rights" by maintaining an "unconstitutional, inferior, and discriminatory status for same-sex couples." With a nod to *Brown v. Board of Education*, the court said, "The history of our nation has demonstrated that separate is seldom, if ever, equal. The dissimilitude between the terms 'civil marriage' and 'civil union' is not innocuous; it is a considered choice of language that reflects a demonstrable assigning of same-sex, largely homosexual, couples to second-class status."[6]

While Massachusetts was on its way to becoming the first state in the nation to legalize same-sex marriage, gay rights organizations and social conservative groups in other states were mobilizing for battle in the legislatures and the courts. Georgia conservatives wanted to block the Georgia Supreme Court from legalizing same-sex marriage and recognizing same-sex marriages from other jurisdictions. The state legislature had already defined marriage as "a union only of man and woman" in a 1996 law, but it would take a constitutional amendment to disable the court's ability to declare unconstitutional the statutory ban against same-sex marriage.

After months of lobbying, emotional debate, and a raucous mass demonstration at the state capitol, the Republican-authored resolution to add a same-sex marriage ban to the Georgia Constitution passed with the necessary two-thirds majority in both the Senate and House. The initiative had earned a place on the November ballot, and Sears's battle against Brantley would be a preview of the struggle to come. The hot-button issue's potential to derail Sears's candidacy prompted a cautiously neutral response when she was endorsed by Georgia Equality, the state's largest gay rights group. "It was not solicited. It is not unwelcome," she commented. She deflected Brantley's accusation that she was a supporter of gay marriage by pointing out that the court had never been presented with a case addressing the subject and that Georgia voters would soon decide whether there should be a state constitutional amendment banning same-sex unions.[7]

Brantley's claim to be a conservative candidate more in tune with Georgia's values also led Sears to dissuade her younger brother from stumping for her campaign. Michael, now a lawyer living in California, was appalled that the governor had injected himself into the race. When Michael offered to travel to Georgia with some friends from San Francisco to support her candidacy, Sears declined. "You know, the one thing I *don't* need right now is a whole bunch of people from San Francisco," she laughed. The city's status as a gay mecca might mean that their presence would do her more harm than good among generally conservative Georgians.[8]

Another issue that came to figure prominently in campaign attacks was the "rule of lenity," a judicial doctrine applied by a court when it must interpret conflicting statutes that subject one criminal act to two different penalties. According to the rule, ambiguities are to be resolved in favor of the defendant. Sears had voted with the majority in a recent nationally publicized case that involved Marcus Dixon, an eighteen-year-old black male who had sexual intercourse with a fifteen-year-old white female. He had been acquitted of rape but convicted of both misdemeanor statutory rape (nonforced sex with a minor, who is not considered able to give consent) and felony child molestation. The court found that the legislature had intended to punish sex between teenagers less than three years apart as a misdemeanor, so it reversed the child molestation conviction. A pair of *Atlanta Journal-Constitution* columnists brought up the case and the rule of lenity in an attempt to illustrate one problem with unfettered campaign speech in a judicial race. They predicted that campaign rhetoric would distill the case into an accusation that Sears voted to set an African American man free after he was convicted of molesting a young white girl, noting, "There's not a bumper sticker big enough" to explain the complicated legal reasoning behind the opinion. Indeed, Brantley accused Sears of being a liberal, activist judge who had joined an opinion he viewed as having been written to justify a predetermined result.[9]

Many commentators opined that the term *judicial activism* was virtually meaningless. "As nearly as we can tell, a 'judicial activist' jurist is one who rules against your wishes. . . . In other words, judicial activism is like beauty; it is in the eye of the beholder," wrote pundit Bill Shipp. There is no general consensus regarding what the term means, though it is often coupled with the word *liberal* and used as a pejorative. The epithet is sometimes invoked to describe jurists who issue opinions that overrule acts of other branches of government (or court precedents) because of their personal beliefs, irrespective of the law. However, it is often used in a looser sense to describe a jurist who incorrectly interprets the law because of a personal agenda. Since the core function of a court is to interpret law, which includes striking down unconstitutional acts, statutes, or precedent, Shipp's comment cut to the heart of the matter: whether an exercise of judicial power is deemed legitimate or not often depends on whose ox is being gored. As Sears remarked to a reporter, "We don't like to say that [we make] the law, but we do that when there are conflicts in the law; when we declare laws unconstitutional or constitutional through our various interpretations." She cited *Brown v. Board of Education* as an example of how the U.S. Supreme Court made law when it struck down state-sponsored segregation in public schools, explaining "We do the same thing here with Federal Laws and State laws."[10]

Brantley supporter and former Georgia attorney general Michael Bowers charged Sears with judicial activism when she opined that the electric chair was cruel and unusual punishment. However, as one article pointed out, Sears voted with a 4–3 majority when the issue reached the court, many other state high courts had come to the same conclusion, and she wrote a concurring opinion to emphasize that punishment by death—for example, by lethal injection—remained an option under the law. "If she's an activist, then so is the majority of other justices who've sided with her about 95 percent of the time," editorialized the *Savannah Morning News*. In the opinion of the paper's editors, Sears's real transgression in the eyes of her Republican critics was that she had sided with the majority when it found in favor of the attorney general in *Perdue v. Baker*—a decision that the editors believed represented a correct interpretation of the separation of powers.[11]

This was hardly the first time Sears had been branded a liberal, though legal analysts generally agreed that she defied easy categorization. She was quick to point out that her personal life belied that label. Sears had been born on a military base, and her father was a lieutenant colonel in the army. Her mother was a retired teacher, and her daughter attended Southwest Atlanta Christian Academy, where, according to Sears, the students "pray and praise every morning." She had voted for both Republicans and Democrats, nationally and locally. Sears also denied that her professional life revealed a particular political persuasion. She termed herself a judicial moderate, a fiscal conservative, and a civil libertarian. She acknowledged that she was strongly protective of individual autonomy, freedom of choice, and privacy rights but pointed out that she had also written and joined many probusiness opinions and had affirmed the vast majority of the death penalty cases that reached the Supreme Court. Her campaign appearances were not restricted to Democratic or Republican functions; she was as willing to speak to a Republican women's group in Cobb County as she was to participate in a house party for a crowd of Democratic contributors. As she said, "I still consider myself nonpartisan." The *Atlanta Journal-Constitution* observed that Sears, who was running against the politicization of judicial races, was engaged in a delicate balancing act.[12]

Brantley's campaign got off to a rocky start when it was discovered that ten liens had been placed on his residence for several years' worth of unpaid bills, including unemployment insurance premiums, employee income tax withholding, and fees to his homeowners association. Brantley had settled most of the claims shortly before he qualified as a candidate in May, and he blamed the liens on "reliance on an aide, a dispute and plain forgetfulness." In addition, Brantley's fliers and his campaign and law firm websites erroneously claimed that he had been nominated to the federal bench by President George H. W. Bush in 1992. In reality, a local Republican patronage committee had recommended Brantley and another attorney, Christopher Hagy, for two vacancies on the U.S. District Court. Bush had nominated Hagy by sending his name to the Senate Judiciary Committee but did not nominate Brantley before losing to Bill Clinton in the 1992 presidential election. Brantley retracted his claim, acknowledging the difference between a nomination and a recommendation and labeling the reference "inartful."[13]

Sears ran television ads attacking Brantley on both fronts. Brantley mailed out material accusing Sears of supporting gay marriage and noting that she had been endorsed by Georgia Equality, an organization devoted to ensuring civil rights for members of the LGBT community. Brantley collected endorsements from thirty of Georgia's forty-nine district attorneys. Sears was endorsed by seven retired state Supreme Court justices, the Georgia AFL-CIO, and the Georgia Association of Educators. Days before the July 20 election, the Georgia Republican Party e-mailed its members a "special alert" advocating votes for Brantley. Governor Perdue recorded an endorsement that was distributed via automated telephone calls. Shirley Franklin, not only Atlanta's first female mayor but also the first black woman elected mayor of a major southern city, countered Perdue's endorsement with an automated phone call supporting Sears. And although campaign finance law prohibited political parties from contributing more than five thousand dollars to a single candidate in a primary election, the state Democratic Party spent $150,000 to purchase television ads supporting Sears, circumventing the law by adding fine-print endorsements for state representatives Kathy Ashe and Billy Mitchell so that the ads qualified as supporting multiple candidates. Brantley's campaign manager, Paul Bennecke, responded to the ad by sending an e-mail blast accusing Sears of lying when she said she was running as an independent. Democratic Party chair Bobby Kahn retorted that the party jumped in to help Sears "only after it became necessary." Months later, a state GOP leader filed a complaint charging state Democrats and Sears with having violated ethics laws with the ads: neither Ashe nor Mitchell had opposition in the primaries or the general election, and the ads ran in TV markets in which neither representative was a candidate. The Georgia Committee for Ethical Judicial Campaigns ultimately criticized the ads for violating the spirit of the campaign finance law, but the State Ethics Commission dismissed the complaint along with a case involving an identical issue with a campaign advertisement for Governor Perdue. The campaign contributions law was too ambiguous for the commission to find a violation under the circumstances, said one commissioner, and the advertisements satisfied the language requiring the expenditure be for a "group of named candidates."[14]

Sears crushed Brantley, winning more than 62 percent of the vote. But state judicial politics had changed forever. The 2002 federal cases had opened a partisan Pandora's box, transforming judicial elections into "loud and vicious fights, fueled by money, venom and television." Special interest group litmus tests, skyrocketing campaign spending, and political party involvement subsequently butted heads with the ideal of a fair, impartial, independent judiciary. Nationwide, women on state supreme courts were seen as particularly vulnerable to political attack. Sears's sole female colleague on the Supreme Court, Carol Hunstein, faced similar opposition during her 2006 reelection bid. Republican challenger J. Michael Wiggins labeled Hunstein—a generally pro-government, pro-prosecution fourteen-year court veteran—a liberal, activist, soft-on-crime judge and called the judiciary the final frontier to be vanquished now that conservative Republicans had wrested control of the legislative and executive branches.[15]

Hunstein, who was not publicly affiliated with any political party, declined to accept donations from either the Democrats or the Republicans. In contrast, the state GOP devoted more than $1 million to Wiggins's campaign, and Governor Perdue campaigned on the candidate's behalf. Wiggins was also backed by the Safety and Prosperity Coalition, an organization devoted to preserving limited liability for businesses. Bankrolled by insurance companies and the medical industry, the organization drummed up $1.6 million to spend on advertisements on his behalf. Hunstein, alarmed at the potential for partisan and special interest group money to corrupt the court, asserted that her reelection was important to maintain judicial independence in Georgia. She racked up numerous endorsements from legal entities and newspapers and hit back hard with $990,000 in ads, the most notable of which exposed an intrafamily lawsuit and accused Wiggins of threatening to kill his sister. Like, Sears, Hunstein won handily, taking 63 percent of the vote and interpreting the result as a message from the voters that seats on the Georgia Supreme Court were not for sale. "It was just a rank [partisan] attempt to get power; to come in and take control over the judicial branch," commented a disgusted Sears, adding that she found the idea of Hunstein as a "liberal, activist judge" laughable: "Nothing could be further from the truth. And I do wonder why they keep picking women to run against. I don't know if other people notice that trend as well." Indeed they did: in the previous election cycle, nine of the twenty-nine women judges running for reelection in Georgia faced competition, while only six of the ninety-eight male incumbents did so. In light of the changing nature of judicial elections, ignoring an opponent's attacks amounted to political suicide. In Sears's view, "You want to fight back properly. . . . You don't want to be a Pollyanna." Sears had settled on a "hybrid strategy" for her 2004 reelection campaign. She had emphasized her credentials, crisscrossed the state shaking hands and attending church services, and rejected suggestions that she publicly denounce gay marriage and tout her record of affirming death sentences. However, she allowed the Democratic Party to pay for the last-minute ads to support her candidacy.[16]

Sears interpreted the 2004 election results as a triumph for judicial integrity and autonomy. Because voters had "heard and heeded our message, future judges will continue to decide cases based on the law and the facts rather than opinion polls or questionnaires," she declared at her postelection celebration. Sears, resplendent in a striking red gown, beamed at seventeen-year-old Brennan, who had single-handedly planned the gala at Alston & Bird, Sears's old law firm. Sears, a serious fashionista, often selected her outfits to convey a message, and this dress was no exception: she intended it as a proud, purposeful declaration of victory. Surveying the crowd, she declared, "This night Georgians have said that we want judges who are free and independent, rather than judges beholden to special interest groups or judges who have committed to ruling in a certain way on the divisive hot [button] issues of the day. We are all winners tonight."[17]

But timing is everything, of course. If Georgia's 2004 judicial elections had occurred during the November general election rather than in the July primary, the outcome might have been different. Until the mid-twentieth century, Georgia, like most of the rest of the South, had been firmly controlled by the Democratic Party. Between 1872 and 2002, for example, no Republican won election to Georgia's governorship, and between 1873 and 1980, both of the state's U.S. senators were Democrats. In the wake of the civil rights movement, however, the national Democratic Party became more receptive to the claims of African Americans, and white southerners began defecting to the Republicans, who were also more conservative on other social issues such as same-sex marriage. Former governor Zell Miller, who gave the keynote speech at the Democratic National Convention in 1992, the same year he appointed Sears to the Supreme Court, had won election to the U.S. Senate in 2000 as a Democrat but endorsed Republican president George W. Bush's 2004 reelection bid and was slated to be a keynote speaker at the Republican National Convention. In addition, the November 2004 ballot contained a proposed amendment to the Georgia Constitution that would ban gay marriage and was expected to radically increase voter turnout among religious conservatives—almost exclusively Republicans. To that end, the Christian Coalition was conducting voter registration drives and featuring the issue in its voter guide. Georgia's only openly gay state legislator, Representative Karla Drenner, led the fight against the amendment, spearheading the formation of the Georgians Against Discrimination coalition. Also at issue was the wording on the touch-screen ballot: "Shall the Constitution be amended so as to provide that this state shall recognize as marriage only the union of man and woman?" Though that language had been culled from subparagraph (a) of the proposed constitutional amendment, it failed to reflect subparagraph (b). The entirety of the amendment read,

(a) This state shall recognize as marriage only the union of man and woman. Marriages between persons of the same sex are prohibited in this state.

(b) No union between persons of the same sex shall be recognized by this state as entitled to the benefits of marriage. This state shall not give effect to any public act, record, or judicial proceeding of any other state or jurisdiction respecting a relationship between persons of the same sex that is treated as a marriage under the laws of such other state or jurisdiction. The courts of this state shall have no jurisdiction to grant a divorce or separate maintenance with respect to any such relationship or otherwise to consider or rule on any of the parties' respective rights arising as a result of or in connection with such relationship.

Opponents of the measure contended that the ballot was misleading: voters who opposed same-sex marriage but supported same-sex civil unions and contractual agreements might not realize that a vote for the amendment could prohibit the courts from considering cases arising from same-sex relationships such as disputes involving hospital visitation rights, adoption rights, parental rights, and domestic partner benefits. "If Georgia voters knew this not only would exclude same-sex couples from marriage, but also exclude them from legal protection and benefits for their relationships, they would vote against it," asserted a staff attorney for the state American Civil Liberties Union, which was considering a legal challenge. Two *Atlanta Journal-Constitution* columnists mused, "A lawsuit filed in Fulton County Superior Court—for it would be a state matter, not a federal one—would [inevitably] be appealed to the seven-member Georgia Supreme Court. And one wonders what a particular justice named Sears, accused by the Christian Coalition this summer of supporting gay marriage, would do when the case file comes her way."[18]

As the columnists predicted, Sears and the other justices had the opportunity to ponder the question. On September 16, the Georgia American Civil Liberties Union, Alston & Bird, and Lambda Legal, a national legal organization that advocates on behalf of LGBT civil rights, filed a lawsuit to stop the proposed amendment's inclusion on the November ballot on the grounds that it was deceptive and that by addressing not only same-sex marriage but also civil unions and domestic partnerships, it violated the Georgia Constitution's rule requiring that ballot initiatives and legislation address only one issue at a time. The Fulton County Superior Court dismissed the complaint, holding that it lacked jurisdiction to hear the case. The Georgia Supreme Court agreed, affirming that the judiciary could not decide on the constitutionality of the amendment until it was enacted. According to the court, the ballot initiative was part of the legislative process, which could not be challenged until it was complete. Sears disagreed, writing,

> The Single Subject Rule's purpose . . . is intended to prevent ballot initiatives that seek to amend the Constitution in multiple ways within the scope of a single measure. Faced with such a measure, voters are confronted with several different subjects about which they may hold sincere yet opposing points of view, but for which they may cast only one vote. . . .
>
> [A] violation of the Single Subject Rule adversely impacts Georgia's voters regardless of whether the ballot measure at issue succeeds or fails. In either instance, those Georgia voters who are torn between divergent opinions regarding various subjects contained in a multiple-subject amendment measure will encounter the unconstitutionally coercive dilemma of being forced to choose between their deeply-held convictions regarding one subject and their equally sincere views regarding one or more other subjects contained

in the proposal. This is the very evil against which the Single Subject Rule is aimed. . . .

. . . When separate and distinct questions are combined into one ballot measure, the method of submitting the measure to voters is patently unconstitutional. Worse yet, it creates a palpable risk that "no true expression of the will of the people can be obtained" through the election process. . . .

. . . Georgia's voters will suffer harm on election day. Even worse, our democratic electoral processes will be badly stained. I cannot participate in such a decision, and I cannot sanction such a result.[19]

On October 29, just four days before the election, the *Atlanta Journal-Constitution* published a letter from Tess Fields, the daughter of Georgia Christian Coalition leader Sadie Fields. Tess, an Oregon resident who had given birth to a child she was raising with her lesbian partner, had resisted joining the debate until Sadie published an opinion piece in the paper condemning same-sex marriage as continuing the trend toward separating marriage from parenthood: "In no way should we allow the state to give its imprimatur to a lifestyle that is contrary to that which is in the best interests of society as a whole." Tess responded by condemning her mother's "bigotry" and "hostility toward gay and lesbian people" and urged Georgians to vote against the amendment.[20]

The November 2 turnout broke a record, as more than 3.2 million of the state's 4.2 million registered voters cast ballots—approximately three times as many as had turned out for the July primaries. Republicans took the state House of Representatives, giving the GOP control of the governor's office and both houses of the legislature for the first time in 130 years, and the amendment to ban same-sex marriage passed with well over 70 percent of the vote. Similar ballot initiatives were approved in Arkansas, Kentucky, Michigan, Mississippi, Montana, North Dakota, Ohio, Oklahoma, Oregon, and Utah. And President Bush's reelection victory was thought to have been assisted by voter concerns about gay marriage in battleground states.[21]

"It's wrong to put a fundamental human right up for a popular vote," stated Matt Foreman, the executive director of the National Gay and Lesbian Task Force. "We're confident in the end, the Bill of Rights will secure for gay people the freedom to marry." Lambda Legal, the state chapter of the American Civil Liberties Union, and Alston & Bird announced their intention to file a lawsuit asking the court to strike down the amendment. That court battle took more than a year and a half and ended with the Supreme Court of Georgia unanimously deciding that the first sentence of subparagraph (b) did not violate the state constitution, which was the only argument brought up on appeal. According to the court, because the amendment sought to reserve "marriage and its attendant benefits to unions of man and woman," the language was not "dissimilar and discordant" with that objective. "The scope of this appeal is narrow," the ruling continued. "We are not presented with any issue regarding the ballot language, and we do not, as an appellate court, judge the wisdom of the amendment." Governor Perdue had threatened that if the court struck down the amendment, he would convene a special session of the state legislature to pass a new amendment banning same-sex marriage to be placed on the 2006 general election ballot.[22]

Exactly four months after Election Day, Sears's colleagues elected her chief justice of the Supreme Court of Georgia. When she took the reins on July 1, 2005, she would become the first African American woman chief justice of a state's highest court. She was ready. When Norman Fletcher was sworn in as chief justice in 2001, Sears was sworn in as presiding justice. The justices elect a chief justice and a presiding justice on a rotating basis to deal with the court's administrative concerns. For four years the two had worked closely together on the tasks for which she would now be primarily responsible: budgetary concerns, dealing with the legislature, and coordinating with the Judicial Council and the Administrative Office of the Courts.

The year 2005 promised significant personal changes for Leah Ward Sears as well. In May, Addison, who had always been soothed by television's Weather Channel, would be graduating from the University of Virginia with degrees in physics and environmental science, and in the fall he would move on to Penn State University to study for a master's degree in meteorology. In June, Leah would turn fifty. And in August, Brennan would start her undergraduate career at Spelman College. Though her daughter would remain close to home in Atlanta, Leah and her husband would become empty-nesters. "I was always the baby of the court, yet assuming a big job, so now I'm feeling as if I'm moving into the realm where the age fits with where the children are, and fits with the job. Things are moving together as they should," she reflected. "I'm at a state where most people are just starting at a job like mine, and yet I'm at the pinnacle of my career. It's a great feeling." Plenty of other women had joined her among Georgia's political leaders. "The face of Georgia politics today is often wearing lipstick," exulted *Atlanta Woman*, noting that Georgia's women would be occupying not only the post of chief justice of the Supreme Court but also the positions of public service commissioner, house majority leader, and secretary of state. Sears observed that when she found time to go to the nail salon, she frequently ran into powerful women such as Mayor Shirley Franklin, and in the time-honored tradition of men concluding business deals on golf courses, the women would collaborate on ideas while getting their manicures. Such informal connections are particularly relevant to women of color in the legal profession, 62 percent of whom felt excluded from formal and informal networking opportunities in 2007.[23]

On June 28, 2005, Sears was sworn in as chief justice and Hunstein became presiding justice at a joint investiture. Not atypically, Sears's portion of the event generated controversy. She had asked two very well-known people who had played major roles in her life to take part in the ceremony: one, former U.S. ambassador to the United Nations and Atlanta mayor Andrew Young, was a lion of the civil rights era and had served as one of her mentors; the other, U.S. Supreme Court justice Clarence Thomas, was a conservative icon and a friend of Sears's for more than a decade. In 1992, Thomas had read about the political attacks on Sears and had called to introduce himself and to commiserate. She was touched by his gesture of support. They met in person during the summer of 1993, when Thomas dropped by her office, still on crutches after injuring his left foot while playing basketball with his law clerks in the gym on the fifth floor of the U.S. Supreme Court Building (nicknamed the Highest Court in the Land). Thomas and Sears had more in common than their ability to generate a political maelstrom: Sears's family home in Savannah was just a few miles away from Thomas's hometown, Pin Point, Georgia. Thomas found Sears to be gracious, warm, and engaging, and Sears liked him as well. "I don't necessarily agree with him all the time, nor he me. But I'm a judge. And judges aren't supposed to [agree all the time]! I don't like all that my colleagues here have to say. We dissent *vigorously*, but they're my friends." Sears's choice of guests for her swearing-in was consistent with her views of herself as "crossing the lines," bridging gaps between disparate entities: Republican and Democrat, liberal and conservative, black and white. Sears had always had the ability to empathize with people on all sides of an equation, an increasingly rare skill in American society. She wanted the event to model inclusivity.[24]

Perdue did not attend Sears's swearing-in, citing prior commitments—to travel to North Georgia to visit a Georgia Bureau of Investigation crime lab open house, a Chamber of Commerce, and a local industry. Some of Sears's supporters avoided her investiture as well. The Reverend Joseph Lowery, who with Martin Luther King Jr. helped found the Southern Christian Leadership Conference, chose to stay away because of the presence of Thomas, whom Lowery considered "one of the most destructive forces for civil rights and poor people on the court since his appointment." State legislator Tyrone Brooks also stayed away, flatly stating that Thomas was "not one of us."[25]

The investiture participants struck notes of pride, inclusiveness, and gratitude. Thomas seemed to be flooded with emotion as he looked at the euphoric crowd congregated in the state capitol:

> Never during my years in Savannah did I think that I would be in the well of any part of the legislature of the state of Georgia.... This is an especially important day.... Today [is] a day when my pride runs deep as a human being, as a member of the judiciary, and as a Georgian.... Ambassador Young, on behalf of our generation, I thank you and those of your generation who had the foresight, the principles, and the courage to make it possible for us to be here today in our various capacities and positions to witness this historic event.

Thomas paused as the crowd rose to its feet in applause, then continued congratulating the woman of the hour:

> I am confident, having gotten to know you, that you will prosper, that you will excel, and that you will do justice. I know that you will call them as you see them. And I know you will do that well. For those of us who are judges know that it is easy to judge when you already have your mind made up. It is hard to judge when you have to make your mind up.... I congratulate you for being, once again, in the forefront.... I never thought that in my lifetime I would be able to witness a black woman as a Chief Justice of the state of Georgia's Supreme Court.[26]

Young, who delivered the oath of office, drew laughter from the crowd when he obliquely addressed the uproar that Sears had generated with her choice of guests:

I asked Justice Thomas if he would stand with us because I think one of the proudest moments of my life was being sworn in at Jimmy Carter's nomination as Ambassador to the United Nations by Justice Thurgood Marshall. I say that because Justice Thurgood Marshall as a member of the NAACP Legal Defense experience did not agree with civil disobedience and nonviolent demonstrations. And yet we stood there together and carried on a tradition of justice for all America, and we were able, throughout our careers, to disagree without being disagreeable and still be friends. I think I am very proud that Justice Thomas has come to be with us on this occasion, for I think we carry on some of that same tradition. And . . . the fact that Justice Sears has invited her homeboy says that you can't put a label on her, either.[27]

Sears continued the theme of civility and inclusion with her remarks. She carefully referenced male, female, black, and white achievers, acknowledging that she had long ago accepted that her speeches would never equal those of Martin Luther King Jr. or Winston Churchill; her writing would never rival Alice Walker's books or Ernest Hemingway's novels. "But," she continued, "I . . . knew that I could be a good judge, because I loved the law, and I was committed to administering justice respectfully and courteously, and without corruption, greed, prejudice, favor, or affection." She pledged to focus on strengthening the family unit and promoting the independence and integrity of the judiciary before ending by quoting George Bernard Shaw:

This is the true joy in life, being used for a purpose recognized by yourself as a mighty one; being a force of nature instead of a feverish, selfish little clod of ailments and grievances complaining that the world will not devote itself to making you happy. . . . My life belongs to the community, and as long as I live it is my privilege to do for it what I can. I want to be thoroughly used up when I die, for the harder I work the more I live. I rejoice in life for its own sake. Life is no "brief candle" for me. It is a sort of splendid torch which I have got hold of for the moment, and I want to make it burn as brightly as possible before handing it on to future generations.[28]

———————

Sears's torch continued to burn brightly. The media rushed to profile her, and she received countless awards, honorary degrees, and other accolades. She generated headlines by selecting a female bodyguard, Renia Wooten, making the security expert and crack shot the first woman in the state's history chosen to protect a chief justice. She made *Atlanta* magazine's list of "Best-Dressed Atlantans" for the unique vintage outfits she wore to her many public appearances. At every opportunity, Sears wrote about and discussed the glut of domestic relations cases that clogged the courts' dockets, a phenomenon she attributed to the breakdown of the family unit as a consequence of too-young, never-married, divorced, and/or absentee parents. Sixty-five percent of the civil cases heard at the trial court level in Georgia in 2006 involved issues concerning children and families. Sears declared that as a black woman, she believed she was well situated to raise awareness about the social costs caused by the erosion of family and marriage since the problem was particularly pronounced in the African American community. Although almost 36 percent of the country's children were born to unmarried mothers, the figure was 70 percent for African American women. According to Sears, this "intentional infliction of disadvantage" on children resulted in higher crime rates and created huge inequalities and opportunity gaps. She believed that law and public policy needed to play a role in creating and maintaining a functioning marriage culture and established the Commission on Children, Marriage, and Family Law to work toward those goals. She also launched the Committee on Civil Justice to begin addressing low- and moderate-income Georgians' considerable need for legal representation in noncriminal cases, a complement to the work of Fletcher, who as chief justice had overhauled Georgia's indigent criminal defense system by creating a statewide network of public defender offices.[29]

While Sears began tackling her new administrative duties and focusing on her goals, a case that would garner international attention was winding its way to the high court. In 2005, Genarlow Wilson, a star athlete, homecoming king, and high school honor student with no criminal history, was convicted of aggravated child molestation for having oral sex with a fifteen-year-old girl at a New Year's Eve party. Wilson was seventeen years old at the time and the girl, just shy of Georgia's age of consent, was a willing participant. Under the statutory provisions then in place, if Wilson had engaged in vaginal intercourse with a minor within three years of his age, he could only have been charged with a misdemeanor and received a sentence of up to twelve months in jail. However, the "Romeo and Juliet" exception to the statutory rape law did not apply to oral sex, meaning that the minimum mandatory sentence was ten years' imprisonment. Further, when he was released, he would have to register as a sex offender, which would restrict where he could live and allow his photograph and information about his offense to be publicized. Even the jurors who had found Wilson guilty were shocked by the draconian sentence—the consequences of their verdict had not been disclosed to them. The case became a cause célèbre over the next two years, spawning charges of police and prosecutorial racial bias because Wilson was African American. Former president Jimmy Carter wrote to the state attorney general to protest Wilson's incarceration and the "racial dimension of the case." Running for president, Senator Barack Obama condemned the "inequities in our justice system" that put Wilson behind bars. Republican Matt Towery, the author of the law under which Wilson was convicted, denied that it was meant to imprison teens for having oral sex. And since more than half of those between ages fifteen and nineteen engaged in oral sex, the issue of selective law enforcement and abuse of discretion was clearly involved.[30]

While Wilson was appealing his conviction, the Georgia legislature modified the law to make conduct such as Wilson's a misdemeanor and to eliminate the sex offender registration requirement. The modification not only implicitly recognized and accepted the reality of heterosexual teenage sexual behavior but also contained no language regarding gender, meaning that it applied to same-sex relations. But the law was not made retroactive, so the change did not help Wilson. In fact, the General Assembly specifically stated that the provisions of the new law would not affect persons convicted under the previous version of the statute.[31]

After Wilson's appeal had failed and he had spent two years in prison, a superior court granted habeas corpus relief on the grounds that Wilson's sentence constituted cruel and unusual punishment, calling the sentence "a grave miscarriage of justice." The state appealed the decision to the Georgia Supreme Court. By now, the situation had become an "international blot on Georgia's legal system," as one editorial termed it. On July 20, 2007, the court heard oral argument on the case. "Where's the justice?" Sears asked the attorneys, reminding the courtroom that the crime had been reduced from a felony to a misdemeanor, an extremely rare occurrence that indicated the legislature wanted to rectify an egregious error in a law that was intended to target predatory adults. "Teenagers make mistakes," added Hunstein. "Where is the justice in a 10-year sentence and being on the sex offender registry for the rest of that person's life?" Representing the state, senior assistant attorney general Paula K. Smith responded, "It's not up to the Supreme Court to decide where the justice is in the case, or whether Wilson should be released because the law changed after his conviction." Smith argued that the court's only choice was to uphold the previous law that made Wilson's act a felony. "Should we do that at the expense of fundamental fairness?" asked Benham.[32]

Sears agonized over the case while on vacation in Cape Town, South Africa, particularly because the court had just eighteen months earlier rejected a cruel-and-unusual punishment claim made by Joshua Widner, who had also received a ten-year sentence after being convicted of aggravated child molestation. But Widner was 18½ years old at the time of the crime, and his girlfriend was barely fourteen, a gap of more than four years. The "Romeo and Juliet" provision in the aggravated child molestation statute, which became law four days after the Widner opinion was issued, would not have altered his punishment because of the age difference. But since Wilson was only two years older than his victim, Sears concluded that the radical reduction in punishment represented a "seismic shift" in how the legislature regarded oral sex between two willing teenagers. This, in turn, reflected the state's "evolving standards of decency," indicating that society no longer supported such severe punishment for Wilson's act. "At the time Wilson committed his offense, a fifty-year-old man who fondled a five-year-old girl for his sexual gratification could receive as little as five years in prison," Sears wrote. Such an act was "far more serious and disruptive of the social order than a teenager receiving oral sex from another willing teenager." Further, "Although society has a significant interest in protecting children from premature sexual activity, we must acknowledge that Wilson's crime does not rise to the level of culpability of adults who prey on children and that, for the law to punish Wilson as it would an adult, with the extraordinarily harsh punishment of ten years in prison without the possibility of probation or parole, appears to be grossly disproportionate to his crime." Therefore, she concluded, Wilson's sentence constituted cruel and unusual punishment under both the Georgia and U.S. Constitutions. Using the listening and persuasion skills developed over fifteen years on the bench, Sears built a consensus in the *Wilson* case, convincing Justices Hunstein, Benham, and Hugh Thompson to join her in overturning the conviction and ordering Wilson's release.[33]

The decision again resulted in charges that Sears was engaging in "judicial activism" for voting to override the state legislature, and Justice George Carley's dissent accused the majority of "do[ing] violence to the fundamental constitutional principle of separation of powers" by disregarding "clear and unambiguous statutory language." However, other commentators pointed out that it is the province of the judicial branch to construe the law, and even if the legislature explicitly declines to apply a law retroactively, that does not negate the court's duty to uphold the constitution's guarantee against cruel and unusual punishment. This approach comports with the view that the Constitution is a living document, a doctrine that embraces the idea that broad language and ambiguous concepts such as "cruel and unusual punishment" should evolve as society evolves. Consequently, as Sears opined, a legislature's statement of intent that a law is not to be applied retroactively cannot prevent "cruel and unusual punishment" analysis; otherwise, the General Assembly could effectively "dictate to the court when a punishment may be considered cruel and unusual, thus violating the separation of powers. . . . [R]etroactivity analysis [and] cruel and unusual punishment analysis . . . must be, and are, analytically distinct." Although the court could not retroactively apply the changes to the law, it could "rely on that amendment as a factor representative of the evolving standard regarding the appropriate punishment for oral sex between teenagers."[34]

After his release, Wilson met Sears during a reception for his attorney, B. J. Bernstein, who had also worked on the Marcus Dixon case. Sears was both startled and moved to meet the twenty-one-year-old. She rarely had the opportunity to meet the subjects of the briefs she read as an appellate judge, though she always sought to remain mindful of the human consequences of her decisions. He whispered his thanks in her ear and told her that he was about to enroll at Atlanta's Morehouse College. "Give me a hug," she said. "All I want you to do—*all* I want you to do—is make me proud, *please*." Wilson not only promised to make her proud but kept his promise, graduating with a sociology degree in 2013.[35]

Sears's meeting with Wilson particularly touched her because it came at a difficult time in her personal life. Sears's concerns about the societal costs of broken families had been reinforced when her older brother, Tommy, endured a difficult divorce and became a "visitor of his own children." Tommy, like Leah's younger brother, Michael, had earned degrees from the U.S. Naval Academy and Stanford Law School. Brilliant, handsome, and successful, he was beloved by Addison and Brennan, who always knew their "fun uncle" had arrived from Los Angeles when they woke up covered in shaving cream: he would spray it on their pillows as they slept. In 2005, Tommy went to Iraq to work as a lawyer for the State Department and witnessed wartime atrocities, including some against young children, that affected him deeply. When he returned, Brennan noticed that he had changed.[36]

In October 2007, Tommy left the United States to begin a new job in Dubai. On November 5, Leah awoke annoyed at him because she had not heard from him in three weeks. Though usually a reluctant chef, she decided to make muffins, hoping that the sweet smell wafting through the kitchen would restore her normally sunny mood. Still before dawn, the phone rang, and when Leah answered, a woman's voice said, "This is the Dubai Consulate. Are you the sister of William Thomas Sears?" Leah's mouth went dry and she had difficulty focusing as the woman explained that Tommy had taken his own life three days earlier. Leah broke the news to their mother. He had left a note asking his family to forgive him "for the pain that I have caused you. It was not my intent. I now leave to go to a place where there are no tears and there is no pain. I love you all so much. See you soon. Tom."[37]

Tommy's suicide reminded Leah of the brevity and fragility of life, and she began to think about making changes in her own. Her tenure as chief justice would end on June 30, 2009, and she felt that she had accomplished everything she could on the Georgia court. She had for years attempted to answer the question, "Where is the justice?" and she was ready to experience life without having to maintain a "judicial" image. "This is a cloistered environment," she observed, "and I'd like to come out of the convent a little bit."[38]

So on October 28, 2008, just shy of a year after her brother's death and one week before the United States elected its first African American president, she surprised Georgia once more by announcing that she would retire from the court at the end of her stint as chief justice even though her term on the court did not expire until 2010. Obama's election thrilled her: she had secretly pinned his campaign button inside her purse. She was excited about the idea of opening her life to the new possibilities unfolding for African Americans. Obama noticed Sears as well. She was invited to the White House on May 17, 2009, as part of the intense vetting process for candidates to fill the seat on the U.S. Supreme Court being vacated by Justice David Souter. But Leah was not available that day: Spelman College would be awarding Sears, political activist Cornel West, and dancer/choreographer Judith Jamison honorary degrees. Missing the ceremony was not an option for Sears, but not because of the honorary degree. Brennan was graduating from Spelman with a bachelor's degree in political science. Despite promises that she would be back in Atlanta in time to watch Brennan cross the stage, Leah refused to take the chance that she would miss the occasion. Slightly one week later, Obama announced his intention to nominate Sonia Sotomayor to the U.S. Supreme Court. Sears proclaimed the federal appellate judge a "brilliant pick" and carried within her heart the warm, indelible memory of watching her only daughter graduate from college.[39]

Leah's devotion to her daughter was returned when Brennan, who harbors an enormous fear of public speaking, made a surprise appearance and speech at Sears's retirement party:

> A few months ago, when I was getting ready to graduate, I asked my mom, "How do you know when you're in the right job or the right career?" I was balancing the [choice of joining the] Peace Corps or working in a law firm for a year, and I didn't know. And she said, "If you can wake up every day and you're always excited about where you're going and what you're going to be doing, that's how you know you're in the perfect job." And so I started thinking about what I do that makes me happy—that happy every single day, [and I thought about my mom]. She dances in the morning. My mom wakes up every morning at 5:30, the crack of dawn. When she's getting ready, she's so excited about the people she's going to work with, the things that she's going to accomplish throughout the day, and the people she's going to help. And so when she wakes up, she dances. She feels so blessed to be where she is. Thank you for making it such a wonderful place for my mother to be able to come to every day.[40]

In June 2009, Sears danced away from the most productive Supreme Court in the country and one of the five best in terms of national influence and judicial independence. Her final State of the Judiciary address to the General Assembly contained love notes to the state of Georgia and to her colleagues, with whom she had served for so long they could "read each other's facial expressions and anticipate what's coming, sometimes with dread":

> Each of you is a part of my life's story, and I will forever be grateful. . . . It has been a privilege to serve here. But the court, like most institutions, needs constant replenishment with people who are not comfortable with its ways. It is time I moved on. . . . My life has been driven by a desire to do what I can to make things better for all people. As long as God blesses me with health and well-being, I will continue to serve in some capacity. Just as I pledged to Gov. Miller 17 years ago, I pledge to you today: Whatever I do next, I will not let you down.[41]

EPILOGUE

Leah Ward Sears has continued to confound both her critics and her supporters since retiring from the court. Georgia Democrats raked her over the coals for leaving the court a year before her elected term ended, thereby enabling Governor Sonny Perdue to name her replacement. But, as she pointed out, it would have been hypocritical of her to emphasize the importance of judicial neutrality and nonpartisanship and then remain on the court for political reasons. She refused to be indebted to anyone for supporting her candidacy.[1]

Nonetheless, a natural tension exists between the ideal of independence and impartiality as essential judicial qualities and the routes many judges must take to ascend to the bench, and that tension has only grown since *Republican Party v. White* (2002) opened the floodgates to political speech in judicial elections and *Citizens United v. FEC* (2010) lifted limits on corporations' ability to pour money into local and national elections. Thirty-eight states conduct partisan, nonpartisan, or retention judicial elections, and they have become increasingly politicized and polluted by a steady stream of money from interest groups seeking influence. Those dismayed by the state of affairs have launched a range of initiatives seeking to protect the independence of the third branch of government. Since leaving the U.S. Supreme Court in 2006, former justice Sandra Day O'Connor has taken a particularly active role in advocating for judicial autonomy. In 2009, the year Sears left the bench, O'Connor launched an initiative at the Institute for the Advancement of the American Legal System to promote commission-based gubernatorial appointment of judges, with performance evaluations and periodic retention elections. Since 2013, O'Connor has also served as the honorary chair of Justice at Stake, a nonpartisan coalition of more than fifty organizations that focuses on impartial-justice issues through litigation and education.[2]

Choosing to fight unfettered political speech with an informational blitz of its own, the National Association of Women Judges launched the Informed Voters Project, the nation's first fair-courts initiative developed and implemented by judges. The project emphasizes the need for voters to ensure that judges are insulated from political influence by becoming informed about the role of courts and judges and by casting ballots for judges based on their character, work ethic, integrity, and ability to issue impartial rulings based on the law.[3]

In typical fashion, Sears elected to pursue not one but three new paths after leaving the court. She taught a seminar on contemporary issues in family law at the University of Georgia School of Law. She joined a Chicago-based law firm, Schiff Hardin, and served as the coordinating partner of its Atlanta office until 2016, when she moved on to become a partner at Atlanta-based Smith, Gambrell & Russell. Decorating her office is a mixed-media reminder of the childhood days when she fought to straighten her hair, an embellished giclée by artist Leroy Campbell, *Good Hair*. Here, too, she remains a minority: in 2016, the National Association for Law Placement reported that only 2.76 percent of law firm partners are minority women, the "most dramatically underrepresented group at the partnership level."[4]

Sears's third post-judicial endeavor was the nearest to her heart. In 2009 she accepted a yearlong fellowship at the Institute for American Values in New York City. Her work as the William Thomas Sears Distinguished Fellow in Family Law represented her gift to her brother, Tommy. The Institute, with its emphasis on strengthening marriage and promoting thrift, was a good fit for the values she had always sought to promote, and Sears had served as a board member since 2007. The founder and president of the Institute, David Blankenhorn, was dedicated to resuscitating the social role of fathers, a cause that Leah had always championed but that became more urgent to her following Tommy's suicide. However, Blankenhorn was also a prominent opponent of same-sex marriage, and her decision to work with him brought Sears criticism from members of the LGBT community despite her longtime and strong stances in support of gay rights. But as Sears's relationships with Justice Clarence Thomas and many others indicated, she was more than willing to communicate with, collaborate with, and even to befriend people with whom she disagreed in some areas.[5]

In 2010, President Barack Obama again considered Sears for a vacancy on the

U.S. Supreme Court, but he eventually selected Elena Kagan to replace Justice John Paul Stevens. Sears had previously declined to take a public stance on issues that could come before her for judicial review but subsequently acknowledged her support for marriage equality. Three years after Sears joined Blankenhorn's Institute as a board member, he reversed his position on marriage equality: "I do believe, with growing numbers of Americans, that the time for denigrating or stigmatizing same-sex relationships is over," he wrote. "Whatever one's definition of marriage, legally recognizing gay and lesbian couples and their children is a victory for basic fairness. . . . Instead of fighting gay marriage, I'd like to help build new coalitions bringing together gays who want to strengthen marriage with straight people who want to do the same." Sears's refusal to draw battle lines and insistence on keeping open the door of civil discourse no doubt played a role in this change of heart. In 2013, the Institute issued a public statement joined by seventy-five American leaders, including Sears, declaring that it would no longer take part in the debate over same-sex marriage and calling for all people, gay and straight, to work together to strengthen marriage. "I'm pleased with the direction the Institute is taking," Sears wrote to the *Fulton County Daily Report*. "Unlike David, I was never against same-sex marriage. But much like David, I've witnessed the fallout from broken families in the past several decades. . . . [T]he Institute is calling on all Americans to join us in pledging their time, money and best ideas, so that more children in America will be raised in stable marriages that continue to foster the kind of social fabric that makes up America at its core."[6]

In June 2015, opponents of marriage equality lost their fight when the U.S. Supreme Court held that the U.S. Constitution requires states to license and recognize marriage between same-sex couples just as it does heterosexual couples. The Court's words resonated with the attitude that Sears had always taken in her jurisprudence: "No union is more profound than marriage, for it embodies the highest ideals of love, fidelity, devotion, sacrifice, and family. In forming a marital union, two people become something greater than once they were. [The petitioners] ask for equal dignity in the eyes of the law. The Constitution grants them that right."[7]

Sears thus continues along the trajectory she has always followed, working to bring justice to those who need it: from her childhood dreams of becoming a civil rights attorney to her rulings that helped safeguard Georgians' civil liberties to her advocacy for social change as an attorney and activist in the private sector. As her cousin, former Virginia Supreme Court justice John Charles Thomas, put it, these are all "different ways to get at it." And in the words of Cornell's alma mater, *So through clouds of doubt and darkness gleams her beacon light; fault and error clear revealing, blazing forth the right.*[8]

ACKNOWLEDGMENTS

A few years after I began working on this book, both Justice Sears and I lost our brothers. My brother's death, coupled with another loss that led me to a heightened appreciation for my father, caused me to reflect on the importance of the men in our lives. That thought was ever-present as Justice Sears and I discussed Tom Sears's influence on her life, when she wept over the loss of her brother, and while I documented her commitment to the promotion of strong families. And so I dedicate this book about a phenomenal woman to the brothers and fathers who support, guide, and care for us—the men who shoulder responsibility and who are present for us in so many constant and unexpected ways throughout our childhood and adulthood. Dad, thank you for always being there for me, no matter what. I admire and love you more than you can know. David, my "Be Ye Friendly" brother: I will miss you forever. I am so fortunate to have had you in my life for forty-seven years. And to my wonderful brothers-in-law, Richard Spiers and Roy Robert; beloved nephew, Matthew Spiers; and dear stepfather Spike: you have eased the path and the pain and enriched the lives of everyone around you.

And then there are the women. *So* many marvelous women on whom I lean, with whom I laugh and cry, who have supported, consoled, motivated, and inspired me. We have all been to hell and back with each other, a trip made much more tolerable with great companions.

To my mother, Donna Jones, and my sisters, Bonnie Spiers and Laurie Robert: you are the air that I breathe, my sustenance. To my stepsister, Becky Jones: I could not have survived 2009 and beyond without you. Ditto to you, Barbara Scott (my once-cousin and always-friend). And to my stepmother, Cathy Shriver, and stepsister, Debbie Young: you, too, have helped me heal.

Love and gratitude to Barbara Ellis-Monro, my treasured friend since our first day of law school. To my Queens, friends, brunch, and travel companions Constance Campbell, Chris Ludowise, Anastatia Sims, Peggy Hargis,

Sue Moore, Lisa Spence, Fenton Martin, Livia Pohlman Hartgrove, Helena Hernandez, and Carrie Mitchell: I adore you all. Anastatia, you get an extra shout-out for being such an amazing unofficial editor. To Barry, Leslie, and Nella Sharpe: you are one awesome "intact family," and I am grateful to have you in my life.

Special thanks to Georgia Southern University's College of Liberal Arts and Social Sciences dean Curtis Ricker and associate dean Chris Ludowise (double billing!) for always making me feel valued and never wavering in your support and encouragement for this project.

To copyeditor Ellen Goldlust and editor Jon Davies: I am indebted to you for your eagle eyes, perspective, and wise suggestions. And to Mick Gusinde-Duffy: thank you, comrade, for your patience and professionalism, your good judgment and good humor—and for breathing life into this book.

Deep, deep gratitude to Chief Justice Leah Ward Sears for all you have done and all that you are. I am so appreciative of our many hours of candid conversation and the friends and family you made available for interviews. This has been a project of the heart for me.

And finally, congratulations to Fred Richter and Bobby Randolph, who after decades of a loving, committed relationship were finally able to get married in Georgia.

NOTES

Abbreviations

AC	*Atlanta Constitution*
AJC	*Atlanta Journal-Constitution*
BSC interview	Brennan Sears-Collins, interview by author, tape recording, June 27, 2009, in possession of author
CDS	*Cornell Daily Sun*
FCDR	*Fulton County Daily Report*
HSW interview	Haskell Sears Ward, interview by author, tape recording, May 31, 2013, in possession of author
JB interview	Jewel Baker, interview by author, tape recording, August 1, 2006, Rebecca Davis Oral History Interviews, A-2014-054, Georgia Historical Society
JCT interview	John Charles Thomas, interview by author, tape recording, May 28, 2008, in possession of author
LWS interview, June 9, 2005	Leah Ward Sears, interview by author, tape recording, Rebecca Davis Oral History Interviews, A-2014-054, Georgia Historical Society
LWS interview, October 12, 2005	Leah Ward Sears, interview by author, tape recording, October 12, 2005, Rebecca Davis Oral History Interviews, A-2014-054, Georgia Historical Society
LWS interview, March 2, 2006	Leah Ward Sears, interview by author, tape recording, March 2, 2006, Rebecca Davis Oral History Interviews, A-2014-054, Georgia Historical Society

institution of higher learning for blacks in America ("Virginia State University Profile,"
Virginia State University, http://www.vsu.edu/files/docs/university-relations/VSU%20
Profile, accessed December 2, 2016).

9. JCT interview; LWS interview, June 9, 2005 ("slice of pie"); William Harvey Sears—U.S.
World War II Draft Registration Cards, 1942. William Harvey Sears Jr., the Searses' first
child, was born in 1912; Lula Mae Sears, their fifteenth child, was born in 1941.

10. Such sentiments echoed perfectly the values accentuated by post–Civil War "aristocrats of color" portrayed by noted historian Willard B. Gatewood, who stressed the importance of both the formal pursuit of higher education and more informal avenues for acquiring
culture and knowledge such as exposure to books, magazines, art, music, theater, museums, and travel. See Willard B. Gatewood, *Aristocrats of Color: The Black Elite, 1880–1920*
(Fayetteville: University of Arkansas Press, 2000), 255–56.

11. JCT interview; Maurice O. Wallace, *Constructing the Black Masculine* (Durham, N.C.:
Duke University Press, 2002), 11. The black American mason movement had its origins in
1775, when Prince Hall, a free black artisan, and fourteen other free black men organized
Provisional African Lodge No. 1 as part of their initiation into Army Lodge No. 441 by a
group of Irish Freemasons encamped in Boston with the British Army. Provisional African
Lodge No. 1 eventually obtained a charter from the Grand Lodge of England and in 1787
officially became African Lodge No. 459 (Wallace, *Constructing the Black Masculine*, 54–55).
"Ignored by England and denied by their American brethren, in 1827 they declared their
independence from any other governing authority and formed the Prince Hall Grand Lodge.
[A] 'separate but equal' Masonic universe has grown and thrived in America almost since
the nation's beginnings" (Christopher Hodapp, *Solomon's Builders* [Berkeley, Calif.: Ulysses,
2007], 101–2).

12. JCT interview ("recite"); John Charles Thomas to author, June 18, 2008. In 1983,
nine years before Leah Sears's appointment as the first woman and youngest lawyer on the
Supreme Court of Georgia, her first cousin, John Charles Thomas, became the first black and
the youngest lawyer appointed to the Supreme Court of Virginia.

13. U.S. World War II Army Enlistment Records, 1938–46, record for Thomas E. Sears; MS
interview. In 1946, the school's name became Virginia State College, and in 1979 it became
Virginia State University.

14. Morris J. MacGregor Jr., *Integration of the Armed Forces, 1940–1965* (Washington,
D.C.: U.S. Army Center of Military History, 1989), 11–13, 15, 17, 19–20, 34, 36, 47, 50. In 1948,
President Harry Truman issued Executive Order No. 9981, which prohibited racial and eth-
nic discrimination in all branches of the military, ultimately leading to the racial integration
of the armed services (Sherie Mershon and Steven Schlossman, *Foxholes and Color Lines*
[Baltimore: Johns Hopkins University Press, 1998], 158).

15. Mershon and Schlossman, *Foxholes and Color Lines*, 63 ("flying aircraft"); OS interview

("understanding flight instructor"); "Obituaries: Thomas E. Sears," *SMN*, November 20, 1989, SCF.

16. JB interview.

17. Ibid.

18. Ibid.

19. Oklahoma's territorial legislature established the Colored Agricultural and Normal University in 1897. Black settlers raised the funds to purchase land in the town of Langston for the school, which opened in 1898. The university was renamed Langston University in 1941 in honor of educator and public official John Mercer Langston ("Langston University," *Encyclopedia Britannica*, https://www.britannica.com/topic/Langston-University, accessed December 2, 2016).

20. JB interview; OS interview.

21. OS interview.

22. Ibid.

23. JCT interview.

24. OS interview.

25. LWS interview, June 9, 2005.

26. MS interview. Germany was on the front lines of the Cold War, and Berlin had always been a contentious issue between the Soviets and the United States. After Soviet leader Nikita Khrushchev and the East Germans built the Berlin Wall around West Berlin in 1961 and Khrushchev warned President John F. Kennedy in 1962 that he "intended to act on West Berlin as soon as the U.S. congressional elections were over," Kennedy "interpreted the installation of missiles in Cuba as a move preparatory to a showdown on Berlin" (Ernest R. May, "John F. Kennedy and the Cuban Missile Crisis," *BBC History*, http://www.bbc.co.uk /history/worldwars/coldwar/kennedy_cuban_missile_04.shtml, accessed September 18, 2008).

27. MS interview ("Statue of Liberty"); Mark Curriden, "A Jurist of First Impression," *NLJ*, September 6, 1993, 26.

28. LWS interview, October 12, 2005 ("sticking it to you"); Anthony Walsh and Craig Hemmons, *Law, Justice, and Society: A Sociolegal Introduction*, 4th ed. (New York: Oxford University Press, 2016), 362 (1.2 percent); *Brown v. Board of Education I*, 347 U.S. 483 (1954); *Brown v. Board of Education II*, 349 U.S. 294 (1955); Jeffrey A. Raffel, *Historical Dictionary of School Segregation and Desegregation: The American Experience* (Westport, Conn.: Greenwood, 1998), xxvii ("segregation now"); "Bombingham," *Digital History*, http://www .digitalhistory.uh.edu/disp_textbook.cfm?smtid=2&psid=3326, accessed February 8, 2017 ("Day after day"); Martin Luther King Jr., "Letter from Birmingham City Jail," *King Center*, http://www.thekingcenter.org/archive/document/letter-birmingham-city-jail-0#, accessed December 1, 2016.

29. Taylor Branch, *Parting the Waters: America in the King Years, 1954–1963* (New York: Simon and Schuster, 1988), 189, 821, 825, 878.

30. LWS interview, June 9, 2005 ("Children!"); MS interview ("black American").

31. Cynthia Kersey, *Unstoppable: Forty-Five Powerful Stories of Perseverance and Triumph from People Just Like You* (Naperville, Ill.: Sourcebooks, 1998), 159 ("change"); JB interview.

32. Juan Williams, *Thurgood Marshall: American Revolutionary* (New York: Times Books, 1998), 296. For more on Marshall and the NAACP's three-decade legal assault on school segregation, see Richard Kluger, *Simple Justice: The History of Brown v. Board of Education and Black America's Struggle for Equality*, rev. and exp. ed. (New York: Knopf, 2004).

33. *Meredith v. Fair*, 298 F.2d 696 (1962).

34. LWS interview, June 9, 2005, July 20, 2006.

35. Leah Ward Sears, "Daddy's Princess," in *Daughters of Men*, ed. Rachel Vassel (New York: HarperCollins, 2007), 18.

36. Michael Harrelson, Greg Land, Robert Morris, and Dianne Monroe, "Which Way Now?" *Creative Loafing*, April 4, 1992, 17 ("pillow cases"); LWS interview, March 2, 2006 ("your sister's voice").

37. Charles T. Clotfelter, *After Brown* (Princeton: Princeton University Press, 2004), 24–25; OS interview ("look after them"); LWS interview, October 12, 2005 ("Ebonics").

38. Leah Ward Sears, interview by author, tape recording, December 11, 2015, in possession of author ("Niggas!").

39. "1997 Honorees—John Charles Thomas," *Dominion*, http://www.dom.com/about /education/strong/1997/johncharlesthomas.jsp, accessed July 2, 2008; JCT interview ("Whyyyyy?"); Raffel, *Historical Dictionary*, 109; *Green v. County School Board of New Kent County*, 391 U.S. 430 (1968); *Monroe v. Board of Commissioners of the City of Jackson*, 391 U.S. 450 (1968); *Raney v. Board of Education of the Gould School District*, 391 U.S. 443 (1968).

40. JCT interview.

41. John Charles Thomas to author, June 18, 2008; JCT interview; Leah Ward Sears, "Daddy's Princess," 18 ("flew Santa").

42. JCT interview.

43. Russell A. Williams III, interview, tape recording, January 13, 2007, Rebecca Davis Oral History Interviews, A-2014-054, Georgia Historical Society; Russell A. Williams III to Leah Ward Sears, February 18, 2006 ("legacy"); LWS interview, September 26, 2016 ("That's me.").

44. OS interview; Paige P. Parvin, "Supreme Confidence," *Emory Magazine*, Summer 2006, http://www.emory.edu/EMORY_MAGAZINE/summer2006/toc.htm, accessed July 9, 2008; LWS interview, July 20, 2006 ("hair lock"); Ayana D. Byrd and Lori L. Tharps, *Hair Story: Untangling the Roots of Black Hair in America* (New York: St. Martin's, 2001), 47

("preferred look"); Veronica Chambers, *Having It All?: Black Women and Success* (New York: Harlem Moon, 2003), 129; LWS interview, July 20, 2006.

45. LWS interview, September 26, 2016 ("troublemaker").

46. PMY interview.

47. Cord Cooper, "Preparing for Opportunity," *Investor's Business Daily*, February 3, 2000, A4; LWS interview, December 10, 2007 ("not perky); Savannah (Ga.) High School, *Blue Jacket 1971*.

48. LWS interview, November 6, 2008.

49. Ibid.

50. JB interview.

51. Robert F. Kennedy, "Remarks on the Assassination of Martin Luther King Jr.," April 4, 1968, *American Rhetoric: Top 100 Speeches*, http://www.americanrhetoric.com/speeches /rfkonmlkdeath.html, accessed October 28, 2016 ("What we need"); Gary Graff, "Johnny Mathis on the Long Road to Gay Rights: 'People Are Stubborn; There's a Waiting Period until They Catch Up,'" *Billboard*, December 12, 2016 http://www.billboard.com/articles /news/magazine-feature/7617724/johnny-mathis-anniversary-interview, accessed January 26, 2017; Daniel S. Lucks, *Selma to Saigon: The Civil Rights Movement and the Vietnam War* (Lexington: University Press of Kentucky, 2014), 209–10 ("law and order"); LWS interview, September 26, 2016 ("the other way").

52. Lucks, *Selma to Saigon*, 5–7, 77, 203, 208; LWS interview, September 26, 2016; "Final Words: Cronkite's Vietnam Commentary," *National Public Radio*, July 18, 2009, http:// www.npr.org/templates/story/story.php?storyId=106775685, accessed November 4, 2016 ("stalemate"). Although Leah's father was in the U.S. Army, he did not see combat in Vietnam, and both of her brothers were too young to be drafted before the war ended.

53. JB interview ("short"). The emotional connection she developed for creatures in custody would later lead her, as an adult, to volunteer her legal expertise to help establish a sanctuary in the North Georgia mountains for hundreds of chimpanzees "retiring" from biomedical research (LWS interview, September 26, 2016; "About Project Chimps," *Project Chimps*, http://projectchimps.org/about/history/, accessed October 27, 2016).

Chapter 2. An Intellectual Feast

1. Donald Alexander Downs, *Cornell '69* (Ithaca: Cornell University Press, 1999), 1, 202; John Kifner, "Armed Negroes End Seizure; Cornell Yields," *NYT*, April 21, 1969, 1.

2. Downs, *Cornell '69*, 3–4, 46–47, 62; John Kifner, "Cornell Negro Plan Begun in '65," *NYT*, April 22, 1969, 34 ("younger members"); "Beleaguered Educator," *NYT*, April 23, 1969, 30 ("changes he set in motion").

3. John Kifner, "Negro Coeds' House Is Target of a Cross Burning at Cornell," *NYT*, April 19, 1969, 16; John Kifner, "Cornell Negroes Seize a Building," *NYT*, April 20, 1969, 1, 77; Downs, *Cornell '69*, 1, 57–58, 167–68.

4. As noted on the website *Digital History*, several "feminist groups emerged during the 1960s among college students who were involved in the Civil Rights Movement and the New Left. Women within these organizations for social change often found themselves treated as 'second-class citizens,' responsible for kitchen work, typing, and serving 'as a sexual supply for their male comrades after hours.' . . . In 1964, Ruby Doris Smith Robinson presented an indignant assault on the treatment of women civil rights workers in a paper entitled 'The Position of Women in SNCC,' to a [Student Nonviolent Coordinating Committee] staff meeting. [The chair of SNCC], Stokely Carmichael, reputedly responded, 'The only position for women in SNCC is prone'" ("America in Ferment: The Tumultuous 1960s," *Digital History*, http://www.digitalhistory.uh.edu/database/article_display.cfm?HHID=381, accessed September 19, 2008; "Radical Feminism," *Digital History*, http://www.digitalhistory.uh.edu/disp_textbook.cfm?smtid=2&psid=3342, accessed February 14, 2016).

5. Downs, *Cornell '69*, 31, 173, 177–79 ("liberate the Straight"), 186 ("Black Power"); John Kifner, "Armed Negroes End Seizure; Cornell Yields," *NYT*, April 21, 1969, 1.

6. John Kifner, "Cornell Negro Plan Begun in '65," *NYT*, April 22, 1969, 34.

7. OS interview.

8. "Osaka World Expo 1970," *ArchDaily*, December 3, 2010, http://www.archdaily.com/93208/osaka-world-expo-1970, accessed February 3, 2017; LWS interview, June 9, 2005; OS interview.

9. LWS interview, June 9, 2005.

10. *Alexander v. Holmes County Board of Education*, 396 U.S. 19 (1969); *Swann v. Charlotte-Mecklenburg Board of Education*, 402 U.S. 1 (1971).

11. "Stell vs. Board Lawsuit Forced Local Schools to Obey Federal Law, *SMN*, May 16, 2004, http://savannahnow.com/stories/051304/2154761.shtml#.WHKT2fkrKM8, accessed February 15, 2017; *Stell v. Savannah–Chatham County Board of Education*, 220 F. Supp. 667 (1963); *Stell v. Board of Public Education for the City of Savannah*, 334 F. Supp. 909 (1971).

12. Steve Crosby, "Macon Mayor Also Speaks at Stadium," *SMN*, September 2, 1971, 1.

13. Joe Ryan, "About 15,000 Skip School in Chatham," *SMN*, September 4, 1971, B1; Joe Ryan, "Protestors Keep Up the Beat," *SMN*, September 10, 1971, B1; "Busing Foes Shift Tactics, Claim Victory," *SMN*, September 14, 1971, B1; *Stell v. Board of Public Education for the City of Savannah*, 334 F. Supp. 909 (1971)("Alice").

14. Steve Crosby, "Macon Mayor Also Speaks at Stadium," *SMN*, September 2, 1971, 1 ("Adjustment"); Neal Maker and Claude Felton, "Marshals Asked at Jenkins High," *SMN*, September 29, 1971, 1; "Student, Driver Injured on Bus," *SMN*, September 15, 1971, D1.

15. LWS interview, June 9, 2005 ("a mess"); LWS interview, December 10, 2007 ("my way"); OS interview ("acted white"); MS interview ("bored").

16. LWS interview, June 9, 2005.

17. Ibid.

18. LWS interview, December 10, 2007 ("loved it"); Charlotte Williams Conable, *Women at Cornell: The Myth of Equal Education* (Ithaca: Cornell University Press, 1977), 32, 113–14, 146–47; Morris Bishop, *A History of Cornell* (Ithaca: Cornell University Press, 1962), 481; Paula Gantz, "Female Studies Program Faces Uncertain Future," *CDS*, Freshman Issue 1972, 38. Cornell's first female student, Jennie Spencer, began taking classes in 1870, two years before the university officially became coeducational (Susan Cohen, "Women Help Shape Cornell's Past," *Cornell Daily News*, May 4, 1976, 10).

19. JB interview.

20. Elaine Povich, "Cornell Dorms, Now Coed, Offer Many Life Styles," *CDS*, Freshman Issue 1972, 19; Elaine Povich, "Cornell Students Facing Housing Shortage Again," *CDS*, August 30, 1972; OS interview; JB interview.

21. PMY interview; LWS interview, December 10, 2007.

22. PMY interview; LWS interview, December 10, 2007.

23. "Jordan, Barbara Charline," *U.S. House of Representatives: History, Art, and Archives*, http://history.house.gov/People/Detail/16031, accessed October 16, 2016; "Shirley Chisholm," *Bio*, http://www.biography.com/people/shirley-chisholm-9247015#political-career-and-african-american-firsts, accessed October 17, 2016; Barbara Charline Jordan, "Statement on the Articles of Impeachment," July 25, 1974, *American Rhetoric: Top 100 Speeches*, http://www.americanrhetoric.com/speeches/barbarajordanjudiciarystatement.htm, accessed November 2, 2016.

24. LWS interview, June 9, 2005 ("six libraries"; "Women's studies"); LWS interview, September 26, 2016 ("cocoon"; "weirdness").

25. *CDS*, Freshman Issue 1972, 8, 26; Leah Ward Sears to author, April 10, 2007.

26. Dennis A. Williams, "Blacks Create Ujamaa Unit," *CDS*, September 18, 1972, 1, 13; Leah Ward Sears to author, April 10, 2007; Barbara Linder, "Ujamaa Ruling Poses Dilemmas for Cornell," *CDS*, February 11, 1974, 6.

27. Dennis A. Williams, "Blacks Create Ujamaa Unit," *CDS*, September 18, 1972, 1; Maia Licker, "Board of Regents Issues Univ. Desegregation Goals," *CDS*, March 12, 1973, 1; Barbara Linder, "Regents Order Ujamaa College to Desegregate," *CDS*, January 28, 1974, 1; Barbara Linder, "Ujamaa Ruling Poses Dilemma for Cornell," *CDS*, February 11, 1974, 6; Barbara Linder, "Cornell Faces Racial Problems," *CDS*, Freshman Issue 1974, 10; Barbara Linder, "Regents Representatives Call Ujamaa Segregated," *CDS*, April 16, 1974, 1 ("Ujamaa is open"); Barbara Linder, "State Drops Order to Close Ujamaa," *CDS*, December 6, 1974, 1, 16.

28. LWS interview, October 12, 2005; LWS interview, March 2, 2006 ("*pissed* passionate"; "the way society worked"); LWS interview, December 10, 2007 ("black table"; "race was everything").

29. David Green, "'Black View' Aims to Be Medium for Minority Opinions at Cornell," *CDS*, November 16, 1973, 7; *Eclipse*, Spring 1975, 2–4.

30. *Ethos* (Cornell University, 1976).

31. Emilia De Meo, "First Female Law Prof. Named," *CDS*, September 28, 1973, 3; Charles Sennett, "Trustees to Hear Presentation on Status of Women at Cornell," *CDS*, February 12, 1974, 3.

32. "Women Level Sex Bias Charges at State Banks, Credit Offices," *CDS*, October 18, 1973, 15.

33. Bob Bernstein, "Men's Honorary Goes Coed, Ending 81-Year Tradition," *CDS*, October 11, 1974, 1.

34. Christopher Tierney, "Conference Focuses on Black Womanhood," *CDS*, April 16, 1973, 7.

35. PMY interview.

36. Lonnae O'Neal Parker, *I'm Every Woman* (New York: HarperCollins, 2005), 9–10.

37. LWS interview, October 12, 2005.

38. In one instance, campus authorities received a complaint about a smell that was thought to be marijuana but that turned out to be black-oriented hair products. On another occasion, a white psychiatrist instituted a medical suspension for a black coed after she had a loud confrontation with women in her dorm over the volume of her music. The second incident led African American students to call for the hiring of a black psychologist familiar with culture and problems specific to blacks (Downs, *Cornell '69*, 57–58).

39. Dara McLeod, "Sears-Collins Tells Women They Should Be Demanding Equal Pay," *Athens Daily News*, November 5, 1992, A8; LWS interview, December 10, 2007.

40. Spencer was not permitted to live on campus and faced the slippery incline several times a day when she walked to classes, so "when winter came—and snow plows were not yet available—she bade farewell to campus life" (Susan Cohen, "Women Help Shape Cornell's Past," *Cornell Daily News*, May 4, 1976, 10).

41. PMY interview.

42. OS interview ("southern girl"); LWS interview, December 10, 2007.

43. David C. Knapp, "Decentralizing COSEP," *Cornell Daily News*, March 4, 1975, 4 ("add-on"); Cathy Panagoulias, "Flashbacks of Cornell," *Cornell Daily News*, Senior Issue, May 1975, 14; Barbara Linder, "LSC Controversy: Who's Committed?" *CDS*, March 6, 1975, 1, 12–13.

44. Sandra Widener, "Blacks Detain President during Protest on Rape," *CDS*, November 14, 1975, 1; *The Cornellian*, 1976, 188.

45. PMY interview; LWS interview, December 10, 2007.

46. Bob Bernstein and David Rosenberg, "Blacks Hold Day Hall for 10 Hours, Leave after Court Order Is Issued," *CDS*, April 21, 1976, 1, 10.

Chapter 3. Love, Life, and Death

1. LWS interview, November 6, 2008.

2. LWS interview, October 12, 2005; LWS interview, November 6, 2008.

3. Martha Rampton, "The Three Waves of Feminism," *Pacific*, Fall 2008, http://www
.pacificu.edu/magazine_archives/2008/fall/echoes/feminism.cfm, accessed May 7, 2014;
Michael Harrelson, Greg Land, Robert Morris, and Dianne Monroe, "Which Way Now?"
Creative Loafing, April 4, 1992, 15; *Our Bodies, Ourselves*, 2nd ed. (New York: Boston
Women's Health Book Collective, 1976), 69–71.

4. "Collins, Sears Rites Held," *Savannah News-Press*, July 4, 1976, 4E; Patricia
McCormack, "The Envy of the Publishing World," *Savannah News-Press*, July 4, 1976, 6E
("baby doll"). The integration of the obituary pages and the "women's section," where wedding announcements appeared, occurred in mid-1965 with "little discussion and no fanfare
. . . when all the editors were called in for a conference and were told that, if there were no
objections, the new policy would be enacted." According to managing editor Tom Coffey, the
newspaper was initially bombarded with calls and letters, but the furor died down within a
week (Sharon Peters, "Integration . . . Change Brought on New Lifestyle," *Savannah Morning
News-Press*, July 4, 1976, 6GG).

5. LWS interview, October 12, 2005; LWS interview, November 6, 2008; LWS interview,
September 26, 2016.

6. Leah Sears-Collins published the following articles in the *Columbus Ledger*: "Bee, Wasp
Bites Deadly for Sensitive Victims," August 21, 1977, B1; "Beware," August 5, 1977, B1; "Far
from Home," July 23, 1977, B2; "Festival," July 3, 1977, C11; "Most Defend Andrew Young's
Remarks," June 13, 1977, B1; "Rats Are Enemies That Don't Give Up," August 10, 1977, A1.

7. Rebecca Zimmerman, interview by author, tape recording, November 2, 2007, in possession of author.

8. Katherine Hanson, Vivian Guilfoy, and Sarita Pillai, *More Than Title IX: How Equity
in Education Has Shaped the Nation* (Lanham, Md.: Rowman and Littlefield, 2011), 10–11;
"First Year and Total J.D. Enrollment by Gender, 1947–2011," *American Bar Association*,
http://www.americanbar.org/content/dam/aba/administrative/legal_education_and
_admissions_to_the_bar/statistics/jd_enrollment_1yr_total_gender.authcheckdam.pdf,
accessed May 26, 2014; Marc Miller, "Georgia's Historic Law Schools, Part III—Emory: The
Creation of a National Law School," *Georgia State Bar Journal*, November 1990, 88. Although
Miller indicated that two students composed the entering class, the correct number is three.
Hugh F. MacMillan Law Library archivist Vanessa King to author, March 16, 2017.

9. *Emory University v. Nash*, 218 Ga. 317 (1962); Miller, "Georgia's Historic Law Schools,"
91–93.

10. Miller, "Georgia's Historic Law Schools," 91–93.

11. "African American J.D. Enrollment, 1971–2010," *American Bar Association*, http://www.americanbar.org/content/dam/aba/migrated/legaled/statistics/charts/stats_13 .authcheckdam.pdf, accessed May 27, 2014.

12. "History," *Hope Harbour*, http://www.hopeharbour.org/#!history/c1i8e, accessed February 14, 2016; Leah Ward Sears to author, May 9, 2014; LWS interview, October 12, 2005; Battered Women Memo, 1980, Sears Papers.

13. JCT interview.

14. JCT interview ("different ways"); LWS interview, December 10, 2007 ("very few blacks"). Alston, Miller & Gaines merged with Jones, Bird and Howell in 1982 to become Alston & Bird. "History," *Alston & Bird*, http://www.alston.com/firm-history/, accessed February 4, 2017.

15. Barbara N. Berkman, "Few Black Partners at Top Firms," *FCDR*, August 3, 1987, 1; LWS interview, October 12, 2005, December 10, 2007; LWS interview, November 6, 2008; Cynthia Kersey, *Unstoppable: Forty-Five Powerful Stories of Perseverance and Triumph from People Just Like You* (Naperville, Ill.: Sourcebooks, 1998).

16. Andrew J. DeRoche, *Andrew Young* (Wilmington, Del.: Scholarly Resources, 2003), xi, 13 ("eye of the storm"), 19, 76, 97–119.

17. LWS interview, June 9, 2005, March 2, 2006; Katheryn Hayes Tucker, "Making History," *GeorgiaTrend*, http://www.georgiatrend.com/site/page7447.html, accessed July 17, 2006.

18. LWS interview, June 9, 2005.

19. LWS interview, December 14, 2006; LWS interview, November 6, 2008.

20. LWS interview, October 12, 2005; Tom Barry, "On the Rise," *FCDR*, August 25, 2003, 5–6.

21. Clarence Thomas, interview, tape recording, May 27, 2008, Rebecca Davis Oral History Interviews, A-2014-054, Georgia Historical Society; A. E. Dick Howard, "Tribute to Justice John Charles Thomas," *Virginia Law Review* 70, no. 5 (1974): 875–77; "Alston & Bird Attorney Sworn-In as New Judge," *Atlanta Daily World*, September 22, 1985, 1; "Collins, Sears Rites Held," *Savannah News-Press*, July 4, 1976, 4E.

22. "Judge Leah Sears-Collins: The Young Judge with Old Values," *Atlanta Bar Association Newsletter*, March 18, 1991, 1B ("Thurgood"); Leah Ward Sears, interview by author, tape recording, December 11, 2015, in possession of author ("[Marshall]"); Leah Sears-Collins, "The Importance of Our Court of First Resort," *Court Review* 24, no. 4 (1987): 10–18; LWS interview, July 20, 2006 ("dress code").

23. LWS interview, July 20, 2006; Prentice Palmer and David K. Secrest, "Candidates Flock to Qualify for Key Legislative Races in Metro Area," *AC*, May 26, 1988, 4B.

24. LWS interview, July 20, 2006 ("conservative clothes"); LWS interview, December 14, 2006; David Corvette, "Ex-Judge Is Winner in Fulton," *AJC*, August 31, 1988, B6; Cord Cooper, "Be Persistent and Work Hard," *Investor's Business Daily*, March 21, 2003, A3.

25. Duane Riner, "Fulton Runoff for Judge Not a Staid Affair: Seen as Power Struggle in the Black Community," *AJC*, August 27, 1988, B1.

26. David Corvette, "Complaint over Judicial Candidate's Use of Stationery Dismissed," *AJC*, August 30, 1988, B6; Duane Riner, "Fulton Runoff for Judge Not a Staid Affair: Seen as Power Struggle in the Black Community," *AJC*, August 27, 1988, B1; "Car of Traffic Judge's Husband Impounded," *Augusta Chronicle*, July 7, 1988, 5B.

27. David Corvette, "Ex-Judge Is Winner in Fulton," *AJC*, August 31, 1988, B6; Thonnia Lee, "County's First Black Female Jurist Declares Scales of Justice Will Not Change with Her," *AJC*, September 8, 1988, D3; Duane Riner, "Justice Is a Little More Blind," *AJC*, December 20, 1988, A1.

28. Duane Riner, "Justice Is a Little More Blind," *AJC*, December 20, 1988, A1.

29. LWS interview, October 12, 2005; OS interview; "Collins, Sears Rites Held," *Savannah News-Press*, July 4, 1976, 4E.

30. "Judge Leah Sears-Collins: The Young Judge with Old Values," Atlanta Bar Association Newsletter, March 18, 1991, B1; John L. Jackson and Elise Rosenblum, "Judges Say 'Briefs' No Longer Are," *FCDR*, August 24, 1990, 4.

31. *Silverman v. Hughley*, No. D-83101 (Fult. Super. Order October 17, 1990).

32. In *Shelby County v. Holder* (133 S. Ct. 2612 [2013]), the U.S. Supreme Court struck down Section 4(b) of the Voting Rights Act of 1965, which contained the preclearance requirement. The Court reasoned that Section 4(b) was based on an old formula that had no logical relation to the present day and that it could not be used as a basis for subjecting jurisdictions to preclearance by federal authorities.

33. Rorie Sherman, "High Court Affirms Sec. 5 of Act Applies to Judicial Elections; Voting Rights," *NLJ*, October 29, 1990; *Brooks v. State Bd. of Elections*, 775 F. Supp. 1470 (S.D.Ga. 1989); *Brooks v. Georgia State Bd. of Elections*, 498 U.S. 916 (1990).

34. David Lundy, "Hicks Qualifies for Appellate Race," *FCDR*, May 1, 1990, 2; Jeanne Cummings, "Miller Tackling Discrimination Suit," *AJC*, April 11, 1991; LWS interview, July 20, 2006.

35. Sandra McIntosh, "Judge Blocks Contested Baby's Adoption; Teen Parents, Agency Pursuing Custody Battle," *AC*, March 23, 1991, B1; Jane Hansen, "Make Adoptions a Non-Profit Affair," *AC*, April 20, 1991, B1.

36. Gina Stappas Gassert, "Court Returns Baby to Parents," *Gwinnet Daily News*, April 17, 1991; Sandra McIntosh, "Infant Returned to Teen Parents in Custody Dispute; Judge: Father Coerced into Signing Adoption Form," *AJC*, April 16, 1991, A1; Sandra McIntosh, "Starting Over as a Family; Judge Rules Father Coerced into Signing Adoption Form," *AJC*, April 17, 1991, D1; Sandra McIntosh, "Teenagers Given Back Baby Boy They Gave Up; Appeal, $1 Million Lawsuit Dropped," *AJC*, October 11, 1991, F6; Sandra McIntosh, "Teens Fighting for Baby's Return; Battle with Adoption Agency Resumes in Fulton Court Today," *AJC*, April 15,

1991, A1; Sandra McIntosh, "Teens Learn Today If They Regain Infant," *AJC*, April 16, 1991, D16; "Judge Blasts Adoption Agency for Refusing to Give Young Lovers' Baby Back," *Star*, May 14, 1991.

37. Ronald Smothers, "Atlanta Court Bars Efforts to End Life Support for Stricken Girl, 13," *NYT*, October 18, 1991, A10; Sandra McIntosh, "Hospital Asks Court to Allow Child to Die; Dad Waiting for a Miracle to Save Girl, Physician Says," *AC*, October 15, 1991, D1; Sandra McIntosh, "Doctors: Keeping Girl Alive Is 'Abuse'; Unyielding Dad Awaits Miracle," *AC*, October 16, 1991, A1; Sandra McIntosh, "Hearing Set on Hospital Request to Cut Girl's Life Support," *AJC*, October 11, 1991, F6.

38. Ronald Smothers, "Atlanta Court Bars Efforts to End Life Support for Stricken Girl, 13," *NYT*, October 18, 1991, A10.

39. Susan Lang, "Alumni Profiles: Leah Sears-Collins," *Cornell Today*, Winter 1992, SCF ("broader philosophical and religious issues"); Sandra McIntosh, "Judge Visits Bedside of Comatose Girl; Jurist Must Rule on Halt to Life-Support," *AJC*, October 16, 1991, A1 ("no more good mornings"); Sandra McIntosh, "'I Don't Believe There's Such a Thing as No Hope'; Father Pleads to Keep Jane Doe Alive; Judge to Rule Today on Hospital Bid to Disconnect Girl's Support System," *AJC*, October 17, 1991, F1.

40. Gary Pomerantz, "Jane Suddenly at Heart of Right-to-Die Debate," *AJC*, October 18, 1991, C3; Sandra McIntosh, "Judge Sides with Jane's Parents; Says Stopping Life Support Would Be Close to Giving Patient 'Duty to Die'" ("This court finds"); *AJC*, October 18, 1991, C1; Sandra McIntosh, "Pain Ends Peacefully for Jane Doe, Parents," *AJC*, October 26, 1991, B1; LWS interview, July 20, 2006 ("keep the family together").

41. "Struggling with the Jane Doe Case," *AC*, October 20, 1991, G4.

42. Bobby Lee Cook to Leah Sears-Collins, October 18, 1991.

43. *In re Jane Doe*, 262 Ga. 389 (1992).

Chapter 4. The Year of the Woman

1. Betty Daniels, interview by author, tape recording, July 13, 2009, in possession of author.

2. Dick Pettys, "Ex-Justice Says Miller Reneged on His Promise; Vetoed Bill Ending Forced Retirement," *AJC*, December 24, 1991, E3; Jeffry Scott, "Served State in Pivotal Posts; Friends Say Judge, Legislator Never Forgot His Roots," *AJC*, August 25, 2010, 5B; Susannah Vesey, "Peach Buzz: The Grass Is Greener beyond the Pasture Gate," *AJC*, March 1, 1992, C1; *Smith v. Miller*, 261 Ga. 560 (1991).

3. Supreme Court of Georgia booklet, Sears Papers. During Leah Ward Sears's time on the court, it had seven members, but since January 1, 2017, it has been expanded to nine justices.

4. Betty Daniels, interview by author, tape recording, July 13, 2009, in possession of author; *Cobb County v. Buchanan*, 261 Ga. 857 (1992); Katie Wood, "Sizing Up Sears-Collins:

What to Make of Newest Justice," *FCDR*, April 3, 1992, 1, 5. When a Georgia Supreme Court justice cannot serve on a particular case as a result of a conflict of interest or other issue, a superior court judge is designated to serve in his or her place.

5. Katie Wood, "Sizing Up Sears-Collins: What to Make of Newest Justice," *FCDR*, April 3, 1992, 1, 5 ("parental anguish").

6. Debra Warlick and Holly Crenshaw, *AJC*, February 1, 1992, B6; Mark Sherman, "Miller May Name Woman to High Court: 10 Finalists for Vacancy Include Only Three Men," *AJC*, B2. All of the sitting Supreme Court justices had declined to participate in the Smith case.

7. LWS interview, July 20, 2006.

8. LWS interview, March 2, 2006; Zell Miller, telephone interview by author, June 12, 2009, in possession of author; Mark Curriden, "Road to a Judicial Appointment Not Clear—Even to State's Judges," *AJC*, December 21, 1992, C3.

9. "Zell Makes History," *Creative Loafing*, February 22, 1992, unidentified newspaper clipping, SCF; "Sears-Collins Appointed to State Supreme Court," *Savannah Evening Press*, February 18, 1992; Kim Madlom, "State Can Be Proud of New S.C. Justice," *Thomaston Times*, May 25, 1992. Juanita Kidd Stout, the first African American woman to serve on a state's highest court, received an interim appointment to the Pennsylvania Supreme Court in 1988 and served until 1989, when she reached the mandatory retirement age of seventy (Robert McG. Thomas Jr., "J. K. Stout, Pioneering Judge in Pennsylvania, Is Dead at 79," *NYT*, August 24, 1998, http://www.nytimes.com/1998/08/24/us/j-k-stout-pioneering-judge-in-pennsylvania-is-dead-at-79.html, accessed January 22, 2017).

10. "Governor Appoints Sears-Collins and Johnson to Appellate Courts," *Voices for Children*, March 1992, SCF; "Interview with the Honorable Leah Sears-Collins," *Family Law Section Newsletter*, State Bar of Georgia, December 1990, 2.

11. LWS interview, March 2, 2006; Coretta Scott King to Leah Sears-Collins, February 24, 1992; Mark Sherman, "Woman Is Named to High Court," *AJC*, February 18, 1992, D1; "Miller Appoints Sears-Collins," WAGA-TV, February 17, 1992, ZM VHS 0282, Zell Miller Papers, Richard B. Russell Library for Political Research and Studies, University of Georgia Libraries, Athens.

12. "Leah Sears-Collins Sworn In by Governor for Seat on Georgia Supreme Court," *State Personnel News*, unidentified newspaper clipping, SCF; Bernadette Burden, "A Justice for Georgia," *AJC*, March 7, 1992, B2; Mark Mayfield, "Justice Gives Ga. a New Bench Mark," *USA Today*, March 6, 1992, A2; "Newest Georgia Supreme Court Justice Issues Words of Wisdom, Love, and Support at Her Swearing-In," *FCDR*, May 7, 1992, B1.

13. "Miller Appoints Sears-Collins," WAGA-TV, February 17, 1992, ZM VHS 0282, Zell Miller Papers, Richard B. Russell Library for Political Research and Studies, University of Georgia Libraries, Athens ("my gosh"); Leah Ward Sears to author, July 29, 2014; Cord Cooper, "Be Persistent and Work Hard," *Investor's Business Daily*, March 21, 2003, A3; Deborah L. Rhode, "Women and the Path to Leadership," *Michigan State Law Review* 2012, no. 3 (2012): 1447.

14. Rebecca Shriver Davis, "Leah Ward Sears: Climb Every Mountain," program for the Eighth Annual Weltner Freedom of Information Award, February 28, 2009, 10; Tammy Lloyd Clabby, "Born Leaders: Marching to Their Own Beat," *FCDR*, August 27, 2007, 5 ("blowing smoke").

15. Linda C. Rehkopf, "First Female Justice Says Age Outweighs Gender, Race," *AJC*, June 7, 1992, D 4; Mark Curriden, "Sears-Collins Making Mark," *AJC*, July 6, 1992, C 3 ("stays late").

16. David Lundy, "Young Politician Speaks Out on Racism, Leadership: L.A. Case 'Indicative of Harassment' Blacks Get," *AJC*, May 14, 1992, K1; Lisa R. Schoolcraft, "Newest Supreme Court Justice Sees Key to Success Is Education," unidentified newspaper clipping, SCF.

17. Linda C. Rehkopf, "First Female Justice Says Age Outweighs Gender, Race," *AJC*, June 7, 1992, D 4; Jack Warner, "Court Upholds Upson Magistrate's Suspension," *AJC*, June 10, 1992, C 1; *In the Matter Of: Inquiry Concerning a Judge Nos. 1546, 1564, 1666, 262 Ga. 252* (1992). A concurring opinion is a separate opinion written by one or more judges who agree with the court's decision but want to make additional points or have a different rationale for reaching the same conclusion.

18. *Batson v. Kentucky*, 476 U.S. 79, 89 (1986).

19. *Lingo v. State*, 263 Ga. 664 (1993). A dissenting opinion is a separate opinion written by one or more judges expressing disagreement with the court's disposition of the case.

20. Charles B. Mikell to Leah Sears-Collins, August 29, 1994.

21. *Davis v. State*, 262 Ga. 578 (1992); Mark Curriden, "A Jurist of First Impression," *NLJ*, September 6, 1993, 1, 26; Mark Curriden, "Rollerblading Justice," *Barrister Magazine*, Summer 1993, 20.

22. Robert Benham to Leah Sears-Collins, October 6, 1994, Leah Sears-Collins to Justices, October 7, 1994, both in Concurrences/Opinions 1994, Sears Papers; *Henry v. James*, 264 Ga. 527 (1994).

23. Frank LoMonte, "The Female Factor," *SMN*, July 6, 1993, A1.

24. Sandra McIntosh, "Judicial Trailblazer," *AJC*, March 6, 1992, A1; J. W. Walker, "Judge Sears-Collins Appointed," *Macon Metro Times*, A1; Ron Sailor, "History to Repeat?" *Creative Loafing*, March 14, 1992, SCF; "Best of a Supreme," *Creative Loafing*, November 6, 1993, 24–25.

25. "Step Up for Georgia Justice," *AC*, June 21, 1992, C 4; Sandra McIntosh, "Judgeship Is 'Something I Always Wanted,'" *AC*, February 18, 1992, D1.

26. Tabitha Meier, "Newest Supreme Court Appointee Is Downplaying Race-Gender Angles," *Tifton Gazette*, April 17, 1992; David Marmins, "Taking the Bench, Hitting the Road," *FCDR*, February 28, 1992, 1.

27. Tom McLaughlin, "Boswell Not Worried about Poll," unidentified newspaper clipping, July 8, 1992, SCF; Paul Kvinta, "How Bigoted Is the Bar Poll?" *FCDR*, August 28, 1992, 1, 3.

28. Mark Curriden, "Election 1992: Judicial Candidates See Lack of Interest," *AJC*, July 17, 1992, 6. The ban on discussing issues was lifted in 2002, when the federal courts declared that

judicial campaigns were no different than elections in the other two branches of government; *Republican Party v. White*, 536 U.S. 765 (2002); *Weaver v. Bonner*, 309 F.3d 1312 (2002).

29. Unidentified newspaper clipping, in SCF; LWS interview, July 20, 2006; Nancy Badertscher, "Mud Flying in Race for Labor Commission," *Gwinnett Daily News*, July 19, 1992; Ken Edelstein, "Sears-Collins Fighting to Keep Her Seat," *Columbus Ledger-Enquirer*, June 12, 1992, A3 ("guess who").

30. Paige P. Parvin, "Supreme Confidence," *Emory Magazine*, Summer 2006, http://www.emory.edu/EMORY_MAGAZINE/summer2006/toc.htm, accessed July 9, 2008; Bill Shipp, "Supreme Court Election Stern Test for Miller," *South DeKalb Neighbor*, June 17, 1992; Susannah Vesey, "Happy Birthday and Vote," *AJC*, June 14, 1992, C2; Maria Odum, "Some Hereby Resolve: Let Plain English Prevail," *NYT*, June 5, 1992, B8; *In re Jane Doe*, 262 Ga. 389 (1992).

31. Mark Sherman and Steve Harvey, "Justice Collins Raises $82,000 in Campaign: Funds Come in from Local Lawyers," *AJC*, June 13, 1992, B7; Bill Shipp, "High-Profile High Court Race: Black Woman vs. Techno-Judge," *Bill Shipp's Georgia*, June 15, 1992, 2; Sandra McIntosh, "Judicial Trailblazer," *AJC*, March 6, 1992, A1; Thonnia Lee, "Making Allowances," *AJC*, February 26, 1992, B1; Susannah Vesey, "Happy Birthday and Vote," *AJC*, June 14, 1992, C2.

32. "For the Highest Courts," *AC*, July 15, 1992, A12; "Our Choices from the Well-Qualified Field," *Athens Observer*, July 16, 1992; "Sears-Collins Is the Choice," *Columbus Ledger-Enquirer*, July 15, 1992, A8; "GAE Endorses Leah Sears-Collins for Supreme Court," *The Update*, July 1992, SCF.

33. Rachel Blanco, "Justice Sears-Collins Defends Short Career in Supreme Court Bid," unidentified newspaper clipping, SCF; Mark Curriden, "Election '92: Keeping You Up to Date—Boswell Has Supreme Goal: Clayton Judge Wants to Sign on to Ga. High Court," *AJC*, July 6, 1992, C3.

34. Paul Kvinta, "Upsets at the Fulton Courthouse," *FCDR*, July 23, 1992, 3; Audrey D. McCombs, "Sears-Collins Defeats Boswell in Judge Race," *SMN*, July 23, 1992, A10; Herbert Denmark Jr., "Political Year of the Woman Is Felt in Metro Atlanta and Georgia," *Atlanta Voice*, July 25–31, 1992, 1.

35. Scott Rafshoon, "Forum Highlights Political Pluses, Pitfalls for Women," *Gwinnett Daily News*, June 5, 1992, 1B ("envelope stuffers"); Peter Lewis, "State Supreme Court—Madsen and Houghton to Square Off in General—Dolliver and Dolan Vie for Other Contested Seat," *Seattle Times*, September 16, 1992, http://community.seattletimes.nwsource.com/archive/?date=19920916&slug=1513453, accessed October 22, 2014; Barbara Madsen to author, October 27, 2014; Guy Gugliotta, "'Year of the Woman' Becomes Reality as Record Number Win Seats," *Washington Post*, November 4, 1992, A30; Peter Stothard, "Feminist Wins Battle against Party Machine," *The Times* (London), April 30, 1992, A1; Maureen Dowd, "The Thomas Nomination; 7 Congresswomen March to Senate to Demand

Delay in Thomas Vote," *NYT*, October 9, 1991, A1. Since 2010, Madsen has served as chief justice of the Washington Supreme Court.

36. Clinton, the founding chair of the commission, initiated the award in 1991 and named it after America's first colonial-era woman attorney (Linda Witt, "Three Little Lines Opened the Door for Women Today," *San Jose Mercury News*, August 18, 1992, L2, SCF). During Clinton's 2016 campaign for the presidency, Sears mused on Facebook that she did not understand why people saw Clinton as cold, aloof, or unemotional. During a reception at Sears's home in the early 1990s, her five-year-old daughter, Brennan, asked Clinton to follow her upstairs to meet her dolls. "I'd love to!" Clinton replied. Wrote Sears, "I could tell then, and I know now, that Hillary Clinton is not a woman without love, compassion and warmth when needed" (Facebook status update, October 3, 2016, https://www.facebook.com/leah.w .sears?fref=pb&hc_location=friends_tab&pnref=friends.all).

37. Tony Mauro, "Anita Hill, Hillary Clinton Rally Lawyers," *USA Today*, August 10, 1992, 3A; David Margolick, "2 Women Take Stage and Stir Bar Meeting," *NYT*, August 10, 1992, A10; Linda Witt, "Three Little Lines Opened the Door for Women Today," *San Jose Mercury News*, August 18, 1992, SCF. Title IX was later named the Patsy T. Mink Equal Opportunity in Education Act.

38. "'Year of the Woman' Is Living Up to Its Hype," *San Francisco Recorder*, August 11, 1992, SCF; David Margolick, "2 Women Take Stage and Stir Bar Meeting," *NYT*, August 10, 1992, A10; Randall Samborn and Victoria Slind-Flor, "ABA '92: Feminism Is the Theme," *NLJ*, August 24, 1992, 1; Linda Sue Scott, "Quayle vs. ABA, Round II," *ABA Journal*, October 1992, 34.

39. "The Year of the Black Woman," *Ebony*, October 1992, 112–18.

40. "A Supreme Judicial Appointment," *AJC*, November 11, 1992, A14. Weltner made national news when he resigned from Congress in 1966 after declining to sign a state Democratic Party loyalty oath that would have required him to support segregationist Lester Maddox's gubernatorial campaign. After serving as a Fulton County Superior Court judge, Weltner joined the Supreme Court of Georgia, where he served from 1981 to 1992. Catherine M. Lewis, "Charles Weltner (1927–1992)," *New Georgia Encyclopedia*, September 1, 2005 (rev. September 23, 2016), http://www.georgiaencyclopedia.org/articles/history-archaeology/ charles-weltner-1927-1992, accessed January 5, 2017.

41. Mark Curriden, "The Changing Faces of Southern Courts," *ABA Journal*, June 1993, 68, 70, 72; Hillary Rodham Clinton to Leah Sears-Collins, June 7, 1993; William J. Brennan Jr., "State Constitutions and the Protection of Individual Rights," *Harvard Law Review* 90, no. 3 (1977): 489–504; *Harris v. Entertainment Systems*, 259 Ga. 701 (1989); *Barnes v. Glen Theatre*, 501 U.S. 560 (1991); *Yarbrough v. City of Carrollton*, 262 Ga. 444 (1992); *Gravely v. Bacon*, 263 Ga. 203 (1993).

42. Don Plummer, "Two Years After Tokars Slaying, Neighbors Say, 'You Don't Forget,'"

AJC, December 4, 1994, J11; Bill Torpy, "Lawyer's Wife Slain Near Cobb Home; She Walks in on Burglary; 2 Sons Escape," *AJC*, November 30, 1992, A1; lws interview, July 20, 2006; bsc interview.

43. Bill Torpy, "Slain Woman Had Hired Private Eye," *AJC*, December 5, 1992, C1.

44. "Fred Tokars Arrested: A Chronology of Events in the Fredric Tokars Saga," *AJC*, August 26, 1993, A10.

45. Bill Rankin, "Tokars Called Police 'Idiots,' Witness Says Slain Wife's Relatives Allowed to Tell of Her Divorce Fears," *AJC*, March 22, 1994, E1; lws interview, July 20, 2006; Bill Rankin and Bill Torpy, "Tokars Found Guilty: 'The Verdict Speaks Volumes,'" *AJC*, April 9, 1994, C1.

46. lws interview, July 20, 2006.

47. *Williams v. State*, 1994 Ga. LEXIS 1204 (1994); *In re Siemon*, 264 Ga. 641 (1994); "It's Just Justice Sears, Now," *AJC*, November 24, 1994, E21.

Chapter 5. Not Yet a Perfect World

1. bsc interview.

2. Ibid.

3. *Master of Laws in the Judicial Process—A Program of Advanced Judicial Education, University of Virginia School of Law* (brochure), 1991–95, 1996–98, University of Virginia School of Law Library; lws interview, November 6, 2008; bsc interview.

4. lws interview, November 6, 2008; "Female Genital Mutilation," *World Health Organization*, http://www.who.int/mediacentre/factsheets/fs241/en/, accessed April 10, 2014; Pam Belluck and Joe Cochrane, "Female Genital Cutting: Not Just 'an African Problem,'" *NYT*, February 5, 2016, A6.

5. Leah Jeanette Sears, "Female Circumcision: Crime or Culture?" master of laws thesis, University of Virginia School of Law, 1995; Linda Burstyn, "Female Circumcision Comes to America," *Atlantic Monthly*, October 1995, 28, 33; Lucy Westcott, "Female Genital Mutilation on the Rise in the U.S.," *Newsweek*, February 6, 2015, http://www.newsweek.com /fgm-rates-have-doubled-us-2004-304773, accessed January 23, 2017. Even though FGM has been banned in the United States, immigration from Africa caused the number of girls in this country who are at risk for the practice to double to more than half a million between 2004 and 2014. Another half a million girls and women in the United States have already undergone the procedure. In 2006, the DeKalb County Board of Health initiated an outreach program when a Somali caseworker learned that women were still being subjected to FGM and suffering infection, pain, incapacitation, and shame. That year, FGM became the subject of heated discussion in Atlanta's African immigrant communities when Ethiopian native

Khalid Adem was sentenced to ten years in jail after he was found guilty of having circumcised his two-year-old daughter. Shelia M. Poole and Brian Feagans, "Trial Sparks Debate in Immigrant Communities," *AJC*, November 3, 2006, 5J.

6. LWS interview, March 2, 2006.

7. *Van Dyck v. Van Dyck*, 262 Ga. 720 (1993); Bill Montgomery, "Ruling in 'Live-in-Lover' Case May Hearten Gays," *AC*, February 11, 1993, F6. The Georgia legislature immediately amended the statute to apply to same-sex relationships.

8. K. C. Wildmoon, "Georgia Supreme Court Rules on Domestic Partnership," *Southern Voice*, March 23, 1995, 1 ("repulsive"); Lynn D. Wardle, "A Critical Analysis of Constitutional Claims for Same-Sex Marriage," *Brigham Young University Law Review* 1996, no. 1 (1996): 1, 8 ("baby steps"); *City of Atlanta v. McKinney*, 265 Ga. 161 (1995).

9. *City of Atlanta v. McKinney*, 265 Ga. 161 (1995); *Shahar v. Bowers*, 114 F.3d 1097 (1997); *City of Atlanta v. Morgan*, 268 Ga. 586 (1997). At the time he rescinded Shahar's job offer, Bowers was having a lengthy extramarital affair with his former secretary in the attorney general's office, Anne Davis. In 1995, both adultery and sodomy were crimes under Georgia law, although in 2003, the U.S. Supreme Court ruled that state laws banning homosexual sodomy were unconstitutional (*Lawrence v. Texas*, 539 U.S. 558 [2003]). Cynthia Tucker, "Mike Bowers: Candidacy at a Crossroads," *AJC*, April 19, 1998, G5.

10. *Christensen v. State*, 266 Ga. 474 (1996).

11. Ibid. In *Loving v. Virginia* (388 U.S. 1 [1967]), the U.S. Supreme Court invalidated laws prohibiting interracial marriage. A person or group not directly involved in a lawsuit can petition the court for permission to submit a brief that sets forth its viewpoint. Interest groups wanting to influence the court's decision often file amicus curiae briefs in appeals concerning matters of broad public interest.

12. Mark Curriden, "A Jurist of First Impression," *NLJ*, September 6, 1993, 27.

13. E. Clayton Scofield III, "President's Report—Gays, Lesbians, and the Atlanta Bar," *Atlanta Lawyer*, December 1996, 3; David Goldman, "Justice Sears Style," *Southern Voice*, February 11, 1999, 1. In 2016, President Barack Obama designated a new national monument at the site of the Stonewall riots, the first national memorial dedicated to the gay rights movement.

14. *Powell v. State*, 270 Ga. 327 (1998).

15. "Best of a Supreme," *Creative Loafing*, November 6, 1993, 24–25.

16. HSW interview; "UCLA Interview in Studio with Haskell Sears Ward," March 8, 2011, https://www.youtube.com/watch?v=NGTyrhHCaUo, accessed February 15, 2017.

17. HSW interview; "UCLA Interview in Studio with Haskell Sears Ward," March 8, 2011, https://www.youtube.com/watch?v=NGTyrhHCaUo, accessed February 15, 2017.

18. HSW interview; "UCLA Interview in Studio with Haskell Sears Ward," March 8, 2011, https://www.youtube.com/watch?v=NGTyrhHCaUo, accessed February 15, 2017.

19. HSW interview; "JFK and the Student Airlift," *John F. Kennedy Presidential Library*

and Museum, http://www.jfklibrary.org/JFK/JFK-in-History/JFK-and-the-Student-Airlift .aspx, accessed April 16, 2014.

20. HSW interview; "UCLA Interview in Studio with Haskell Sears Ward," March 8, 2011, https://www.youtube.com/watch?v=NGTyrhHCaUo, accessed February 15, 2017.

21. Betty Daniels, interview by author, tape recording, July 13, 2009, in possession of author; HSW interview; Tim Daly, "Accomplished City Native Is Spalding's First Black Judge," *Griffin Daily News*, January 4, 1997, 1A.

22. Bill Rankin and Ken Foskett, "Clinton to Appoint Ex-Fulton Judge Hull," *AJC*, May 3, 1997, D2; Cary Grubbs, "Last Week's Program," *The Griffitarian*, August 28, 1997, SCF.

23. LWS interview, July 20, 2006; HSW interview; Leah Ward Sears to author, April 17, 2014.

24. Mark Curriden, "Is Naming Judges Serving Justice? Experts Call Plan to Diversify Courts a Rehash of Racist System," *AJC*, November 29, 1992, G1.

25. Steve Harvey, "Plan to Appoint Georgia's Judges Held Up by Feds: Justice Department Delays Approval for at Least 60 days, Seeks More Data," *AJC*, June 3, 1993, F1.

26. *Brooks v. State Board of Elections*, 848 F. Supp. 1548 (1994).

27. Ibid.

28. *Weaver v. Bonner*, 309 F.3d 1312 (2002); Weaver flyer, Sears Papers; Bill Rankin, "Election '98: Weaver Will Run Ads That Panel Calls Misleading," *AJC*, July 17, 1998, D5 ("Why the electric chair?"); "Stick with Sears," *SMN*, July 15, 1998, http://savannahnow .com/stories/071598/OPEDone.html#.WI4yfX-F_Cs, accessed January 29, 2017; LWS interview, December 14, 2006.

29. Jonathan Ringel, "Court OKs New Election Rules," *FCDR*, September 29, 1997, 1, 4.

30. Laura Brown, "Gay-Baiting at the Ballot Box," *Southern Voice*, June 11, 1998, 1; Peter Mantius, "Court Justice Apologizes for TV Ads in Election," *AC*, December 22, 1998, E8.

31. David S. Broder, "Beware the Court-Bashers," *Washington Post*, July 5, 1998, C7; William Glaberson, "States Rein In Truth-Bending in Court Races," *NYT*, August 23, 2000, 1.

32. George T. Smith, Robert J. D'Agostino, Thomas C. Chambers, and David B. Meltz, "Sears' Opponent Mischaracterized Opinions," *FCDR*, July 20, 1998, 5.

33. Bill Rankin, "Weaver Will Run Ads That Panel Calls Misleading," *AC*, July 17, 1998, D5; *Weaver v. Bonner*, 114 F. Supp. 2d 1337 (2000); *Weaver v. Bonner*, 309 F.3d 1312 (2002); *Republican Party v. Kelly*, 996 F. Supp. 875, (1998).

34. Bill Rankin, "Loser Wants Election Set Aside," *AC*, August 6, 1998, 7E.

35. *Weaver v. Bonner*, 114 F. Supp. 2d 1337 (2000).

36. *Republican Party v. White*, 536 U.S. 765 (2002); *Weaver v. Bonner*, 309 F.3d 1312 (2002).

37. Bill Rankin, "Georgia Supreme Court; a Shift in Philosophy," *AJC*, December 20, 1998, H1; Katheryn Hayes Tucker, "Making History," *Georgia Trend*, June 2005, http://www .georgiatrend.com/June-2005/Making-History/, accessed January 23, 2017.

38. *Fleet Finance, Inc., of Georgia, et al. v. Elizabeth Jones et al.*, 263 Ga. (1993); Tim O'Reiley, "Court Reluctantly Sides with Fleet," *FCDR*, June 15, 1993, 1; Bill Rankin and Mark Sherman, "Fleet's Lending Practices Legal, High Court Says," *AJC*, June 15, 1993, C1. Dicta are comments that go beyond the facts of the case and are not necessary to reach a legal conclusion. Dicta are the views of the author and consequently are not binding in subsequent cases as legal precedent.

39. In *Eckles d/b/a Atlanta Technology Group v. Atlanta Technology Group, Inc.* (267 Ga. 801 [1997]), the Georgia Supreme Court was exercising its inherent power to regulate the practice of law in the state.

40. Ibid. ("I commend the majority's foresight"); Jonathan Ringel, "A Justice Works a Blue-Collar Shift," *FCDR*, June 30, 1997, 1, 7 ("a rare sight"); Jim Houston, "State Justice Sears Runs into a Case of Voodoo Here," *Columbus Ledger-Enquirer*, July 24, 1997, A1, A10 ("small differences").

41. LWS interview, July 20, 2006; Leah Ward Sears, "Let's Hear It for Stepfathers, Too," *CNN*, http://www.cnn.com/2010/OPINION/06/18/sears.stepfathers.day/, accessed June 10, 2014.

Chapter 6. A Splendid Torch

1. *Perdue v. Baker*, 277 Ga. 1 (2003); Bill Rankin, "State GOP Goes after Supreme Court Seat," *AJC*, July 3, 2004, A1, A9; Camille M. Tribble, "Comment: Awakening a Slumbering Giant: Georgia's Judicial Selection System after *White* and *Weaver*," *Mercer Law Review* 56, no. 3 (2005): 1065; "Our Opinions: Keep Tabs on Judicial Candidates," *AJC*, April 30, 2004, A18.

2. Tom Baxter and Jim Galloway, "Part 3 of the GOP Trilogy: The State Republican Party Sets Its Sights on a Zell Miller Appoint," *Political Insider* blog, ajc.com, April 28, 2004; Sonji Jacobs, "Group Presses Judicial Hopefuls; Christian Coalition Query Focuses on 'Philosophies,'" *AJC*, May 14, 2004, C1; Walter C. Jones, "High Court Candidate Explains Liens," *Florida Times-Union*, May 26, 2004, http://jacksonville.com/tu-online/stories /052604/geo_15699432.shtml#.WId8mPkrKM8, accessed January 24, 2017; Tom Baxter and Jim Galloway, "Judges Offer No Simple Answers to Questionnaire," *AJC*, June 7, 2004, B2; "Supreme Court Race Pits Veteran Jurists with Differing Philosophies," *SMN*, July 14, 2004, http://savannahnow.com/stories/071304/2299569.shtml, accessed July 21, 2014.

3. Jim Galloway, "Election 2004: Coalition Spotlights 2 Judicial Hopefuls: The Candidates Were the Only Individuals Who Did Not Boycott the Christian Group's Survey," *AJC*, July 7, 2004, B1.

4. "Advice for the Jury," *Rome New-Tribune*, May 31, 2004, 4.

5. Ryan Lee, "Races Solidifying for State, Federal Offices," *Southern Voice*, April 30,

2004; Tom Baxter and Jim Galloway, "Bonds Linking Court Race, Gay Marriage War Tighten," *AJC*, June 15, 2004, B3; Bill Shipp, "Brantley vs. Sears: Conservative Test Case," *OnlineAthens*, http://onlineathens.com/stories/050904/opi_20040509050.shtml#.WI5pCX-F_Cs, accessed January 29, 2017.

6. *Lawrence v. Texas*, 539 U.S. 558 (2003); *Goodridge v. Department of Public Health*, 440 Mass. 309 (2003); *Opinions of the Justices to the Senate, Supreme Judicial Court of Massachusetts*, 440 Mass. 1201 (2004).

7. Jim Tharpe, "Gay Marriage Ban Amendment Passes; Georgia Voters to Decide Issue in November," *AJC*, April 1, 2004, A1; Tom Baxter and Jim Galloway, "Bonds Linking Court Race, Gay Marriage War Tighten," *AJC*, June 15, 2004, B3.

8. MS interview.

9. *Dixon v. State*, 278 Ga. 4 (2004); Tom Baxter and Jim Galloway, "You Be the Judge: How Will the Marcus Dixon Case Play in July?" *Political Insider* blog, ajc.com, May 5, 2004.

10. Bill Shipp, "Are They Running on Irrelevancies?" *Bill Shipp's Georgia*, June 24, 2004, 5; "Justice Leah Sears-Collins," *Atlanta Business Yearly*, 1994, Sears Papers.

11. *Creative Loafing*, July 8–14, 2004, 33; "Here Come the Judges," *SMN*, July 17, 2004, http://savannahnow.com/stories/071604/2307342.shtml#.WJdj5n-F-T8, accessed February 5, 2017.

12. Bill Rankin, "Election 2004: State GOP Goes after Supreme Court Seat," *AJC*, July 3, 2004, A1; Tom Baxter and Jim Galloway, "Election 2004: Campaign Leaders Sound Alarm," *AJC*, June 28, 2004, B3.

13. Walter C. Jones, "High Court Candidate Explains Liens; Grant Brantley Blames Forgetfulness and Other Issues for His Unpaid Bills," *Florida Times-Union*, May 26, 2004, B8; Bill Rankin, "Justice Hopeful Retracts Claim," *AJC*, June 19, 2004, E1, 6.

14. Nancy Badertscher, "Election 2004: High Court Race as Hot as Partisan Battle," *AJC*, July 17, 2004, A1; Bill Rankin, "Election 2004: The Primary: Supreme Court: Divisive Fight Ends in Victory for Sears," *AJC*, July 21, 2004, D1; Bill Rankin, "Court Election, Governor's Race Seed Ethics Feud; GOP Files; Democrats Point Finger," *AJC*, October 5, 2004, D3; Jonathan Ringel, "Democrats' Clever Ad Aided Sears' Re-Election," *FCDR*, July 22, 2004, A1, A3; Scott Simonson, "Sears' Campaign Off the Hook in Two Ethics Complaints," *FCDR*, November 18, 2005, 1, 4. Sears would later enter into a consent agreement to pay $3,100 in fines for accepting several smaller contributions over the legal limit and failing to correctly report contributions (James Salzer, "Sears to Pay Fine for Campaign Violations," *AJC*, November 30, 2007, A10).

15. Adam Liptak, "Judicial Races in Several States Become Partisan Battlegrounds," *NYT*, October 24, 2004, A1 ("venom"); Jill Young Miller, "Supreme Court Race Gets Political," *AJC*, October 13, 2006, D1 (frontier).

16. "State Supreme Court Justice Challenged," *Augusta Chronicle*, October 15, 2006, B5; Stephanie B. Goldberg, "Women Fight to Retain State Supreme Court Seats," *Perspectives*,

Winter 2008, 4–7; Jill Young Miller, "Georgia Votes 2006: State Supreme Court," *AJC*, November 8, 2006, D1; LWS interview, December 14, 2006 ("picking women"); Polly Simpson and Sally Weaver, "Pollsters Want to Seat Far-Right Ideologues," *AJC*, July 16, 2004, A13; Jonathan Ringel, "No Pollyanna," *FCDR*, December 27, 2004, 15–17 ("Pollyanna").

17. Victory Speech 2004, Sears Papers.

18. James Salzer, "Election 2004: Gay Legislator to Lead Anti-Amendment Fight," *AJC*, August 28, 2004, F3; Sonji Jacobs, "War of Words on Amendment; Foes of Same-Sex Ban: Ballot Misleading," *AJC*, September 11, 2004, F1 ("If Georgia voters knew"); Tom Baxter and Jim Galloway, "Gay Marriage Fight on Hold," *AJC*, August 31, 2004, B2 ("one wonders").

19. *O'Kelley v. Cox*, 278 Ga. 572 (2004).

20. Sonji Jacobs, "Election 2004: Gay Daughter Decries Fields," *AJC*, October 29, 2004, A1; Sadie Fields, "The Gay Marriage Amendment: Can't Let the Few Hurt Society as a Whole," *AJC*, October 25, 2004, A11.

21. Sonji Jacobs, "Election 2004 Update: State Constitutional Amendments: Gay Marriage Ban Headed to Court," *AJC*, November 3, 2004, EX14; Cameron McWhirter, "Republicans Run the Electoral Table," *AJC*, November 4, 2004, A1.

22. Sonji Jacobs, "Election 2004: Metro & State: State Constitutional Amendments: Voters OK Ban on Gay Marriage," *AJC*, November 3, 2004, EX14; *Perdue v. O'Kelley*, 280 Ga. 732 (2006).

23. LWS interview, June 9, 2005 ("great feeling"); LWS interview, December 14, 2006; Harriett Hollis, "The New Faces of Politics," *Atlanta Woman*, October 2004, 40–42; Deborah L. Rhode, "The Subtle Side of Sexism," *Columbia Journal of Gender and Law* 16, no. 3 (2007): 625. In contrast, only 4 percent of white men felt excluded.

24. Krissah Thompson, "Supreme Court Prospect Has Unlikely Ally," *Washington Post*, May 10, 2009, A1; "Justice Injured on the Court," *Palm Beach Post*, April 20, 1993, 2A; Clarence Thomas, interview, tape recording, May 27, 2008, Rebecca Davis Oral History Interviews, A-2014-054, Georgia Historical Society; LWS interview, October 12, 2005 ("dissent *vigorously*"); Patrick Jonsson, "Georgia Gets Distinct, and Controversial, Voice as Chief Justice," *Christian Science Monitor*, July 7, 2005 ("stop labeling"); LWS interview, September 26, 2016 ("crossing the lines"). After she retired from the court, Sears underwent DNA analysis that revealed she is 39 percent Eastern European and 5 percent Ashkenazi Jew. She speculated that her genetic makeup combined with her education in mostly white schools may enable her to understand disparate points of view.

25. Dick Pettys, "Sears Sworn in as New Chief Justice," *Statesboro Herald*, June 29, 2005, A5; Ellen Barry, "Thomas Goes Home for Swearing In," *Los Angeles Times*, June 29, 2005, A16 ("destructive forces"; "not one of us").

26. Eliott C. McLaughlin, "Sears Takes Oath, Vows Independence," *FCDR*, June 29, 2005, 1, 4; transcript of Clarence Thomas's speech in possession of author.

27. Transcript of Andrew Young's speech in possession of author.

28. Leah Ward Sears, "Investiture Remarks," *Atlanta Daily World*, July 7–13, 2005, 9.

29. Eliott C. McLaughlin, "Sears Takes Oath, Vows Independence," *FCDR*, June 29, 2005, 1, 4; Gale Horton Gay, "Leah Ward Sears Judges Her Life Good," *Atlanta Goodlife*, October 2005, 15; "Best-Dressed Atlantans," *Atlanta*, September 2006, 64; Leah Ward Sears, "The 'Marriage Gap': A Case for Strengthening Marriage in the Twenty-First Century," Justice Brennan Lecture, Brennan Center for Justice, New York University, February 2007.

30. Tom Baldwin, "Boy Awaits Ruling on Ten Years for Oral Sex," *The Times* (London), June 11, 2007, 7; Wendy S. Cash, "A Search for 'Wisdom, Justice, and Moderation' in *Wilson v. State*," *New England Law Review* 42, no. 1 (2007): 225; Angela J. Davis, "Lawyering at the Edge: Unpopular Clients, Difficult Cases, Zealous Advocates: The Legal Profession's Failure to Discipline Unethical Prosecutors," *Hofstra Law Review* 36, no. 2 (2007), http://scholarlycommons.law.hofstra.edu/hlr/vol36/iss2/5/, accessed January 5, 2017; Siji A. Moore, "Out of the Fire and into the Frying Pan: Georgia Legislature's Attempt to Regulate Teen Sex through the Criminal Justice System," *Howard Law Journal* 52, no. 1 (2008): 227.

31. Debra Hunter and Paul Sharman, "Crimes and Offenses," *Georgia State University Law Review* 23, no. 1 (2006): 11.

32. Jeffry Scott, "Wilson Case at High Court: Ruling in Teen's Case Expected in September," *AJC*, July 21, 2007, B1 ("Where's the justice?"); Brenda Goodman, "Georgia Supreme Court Hears 2 Appeals in Teenage Sex Case," *NYT*, July 21, 2007, 9 ("Teenagers make mistakes"); Maureen Downey, "Wilson Closer to Fateful Ruling," *AJC*, September 2, 2007, C6 ("international blot"; "fundamental fairness"). The writ of habeas corpus is used to bring a prisoner before a federal court to determine if the detention is lawful.

33. *Humphrey v. Wilson, Wilson v. the State*, 282 Ga. 520 (2007).

34. Ibid.; Jim Wooten, "Our Opinion: Court Ruling Is Legislating from the Bench," *AJC*, October 28, 2007, 6B; Siji A. Moore, "Out of the Fire and into the Frying Pan: Georgia Legislature's Attempt to Regulate Teen Sex through the Criminal Justice System," *Howard Law Journal* 52, no. 1 (2008): 227.

35. LWS interview, December 10, 2007; Angela Tuck, "Life after Landmark Case: Genarlow Wilson's 'Road to Redemption,'" *AJC*, May 19, 2013, A1.

36. BSC interview; Leah Ward Sears, "Let's End Disposable Marriage," *CNN*, July 2, 2009, http://www.cnn.com/2009/LIVING/07/02/sears.family.divorce/index.html?iref=mp, accessed August 13, 2014.

37. LWS interview, December 10, 2007.

38. Alyson M. Palmer, "Sears to Return to Private Practice at Schiff Hardin," *FCDR*, May 14, 2009, 1, 10.

39. Betty Daniels, interview by author, tape recording, July 13, 2009, in possession of author; Alyson M. Palmer, "Sears Defends Sotomayor," *FCDR*, June 3, 2009, 1.

40. BSC interview.

41. Stephen J. Choi, Mitu Gulati, and Eric A. Posner, *Which States Have the Best (and*

Worst) High Courts?, May 2008, http://www.law.uchicago.edu/files/files/405.pdf, accessed September 5, 2014; "Chief Justice Gives Her Last 'State of the Judiciary' Speech," *FCDR*, February 6, 2009, 8–9 ("my life's story").

Epilogue

1. Alyson M. Palmer, "Sears to Return to Private Practice at Schiff Hardin," *FCDR*, May 14, 2009, 1, 10.

2. Quality Judges Initiative, http://iaals.du.edu/quality-judges, accessed February 6, 2017; Justice at Stake, http://www.justiceatstake.org/, accessed January 25, 2017.

3. National Association of Women Judges, "Informed Voters—Fair Judges Project," https://www.nawj.org/catalog/community-outreach-programs/informed -voters-fair-judges-project.

4. National Association for Law Placement, Inc., "2016 Report on Diversity in U.S. Law Firms," January 2017, http://www.nalp.org/uploads/2016NALPReportonDiversityin USLawFirms.pdf, accessed February 3, 2017. http://www.nalp.org/lawfirmdiversity_feb2015, accessed October 26, 2015.

5. Greg Bluestein, "Sears Draws Heat from Gay Rights Groups," *FCDR*, May 18, 2009.

6. David Blankenhorn, "How My View on Gay Marriage Changed," *NYT*, June 22, 2012, http://www.nytimes.com/2012/06/23/opinion/how-my-view-on-gay-marriage-changed .html, accessed February 12, 2017 ("a victory"); Institute for American Values, "A Call for a New Conversation on Marriage," *Propositions*, Winter 2013, http://americanvalues .org/catalog/pdfs/2013-01.pdf, accessed February 12, 2017; Leah Ward Sears, "A New Conversation on Marriage," *FCDR*, February 5, 2013, http://www.dailyreportonline.com /id=1202586929843&A_new_conversation_on_marriage, accessed February 12, 2017 ("I'm pleased").

7. The two newest members of the Court, Sonia Sotomayor and Elena Kagan, joined Justices Anthony Kennedy, Ruth Bader Ginsburg, and Stephen Breyer in the majority opinion. The principles the Court cited for recognizing the fundamental right of same-sex couples to marry included safeguarding children and families. "Many same-sex couples provide loving and nurturing homes to their children. . . . Without the recognition, stability, and predictability marriage offers . . . children suffer the stigma of knowing their families are somehow lesser. . . . The marriage laws at issue here harm and humiliate the children of same-sex couples" (*Obergefell v. Hodges*, 576 U.S. ___ [2015]).

8. JCT interview; Archibald Croswell Weeks and Wilmot Moses Smith, "Far above Cayuga's Waters" (Cornell Alma Mater, 1870).

INDEX